Profit Dollars
&
Earnings Sense

Curtis W. Symonds

Profit Dollars

&
Earnings Sense

amacom

A DIVISION OF AMERICAN MANAGEMENT ASSOCIATIONS

Library of Congress Cataloging in Publication Data

Symonds, Curtis W
    Profit dollars and earnings sense.

    Includes index.
    1. Profit--Accounting. 2. Capital--Accounting.
3. Financial statements. I. Title.
HF5681.P8S93   658.1'55   74-28486
ISBN 0-8144-5376-7

© 1975 AMACOM
A division of American Management Associations, New York.

First Printing

Preface

The concept of profit is generally acknowledged as the fundamental role of the free-enterprise system. As the focal point of business management, profit would thus seemingly have one single and agreed-upon definition, one common method of measurement, and one uniform standard of accomplishment.

In practice, however, it seems to be lacking in all three. It not only suffers from a variety of definitions and methods of measurement but also seems to be subject to a wide diversity of opinion as to the adequacy of profit in terms of the financial goals and objectives of the business enterprise.

Inadequate measurements of profit can lead only to inadequate performance in the management of profit. This book is offered as a means of putting each of the profit measurements commonly used in business into proper perspective—a perspective aimed at achieving not only a more complete understanding but, hopefully, a better management of the profit system under which business operates.

—Curtis W. Symonds

Contents

Introduction

$\mathcal{A}$LTHOUGH THE TERM "business" is often used in the generic sense to describe a common grouping of activities organized for commercial gain, it is obvious that no two businesses—even within the same industry—will ever be found to be exactly alike in every respect. The differences, in fact, are often profound, not only in the particulars of product mix, method of distribution, share of the market, and the many details of operating cost, but also in the philosophies, goals, and objectives of management itself. And when these differences are further

[1]

compounded by the more fundamental differences that necessarily exist between businesses engaged in manufacturing as opposed to retailing, as between mining, banking, insurance, and brokerage, for example, it is apparent that business per se is no more than a heterogeneous collection of diverse commercial activities that have very little in common insofar as the tactical details of operations are concerned.

And yet, with the single assumption that these activities are all operating under a free-enterprise system, all businesses and all business management will readily agree that they have one thing clearly in common: *the objective of earning a profit.* Despite the substantial differences that obviously exist from one type of business to the next, and despite the many different approaches taken by the management of even those companies engaged in closely related fields of commercial activity, all business subscribes to the proposition that these are but separate paths to the same goal, and that the end result is clearly the common goal of profit. In spite of occasional disclaimers to the contrary, the profit motive is thus readily established as the single common denominator of the free-enterprise system, the ultimate focal point of all business management.

With this common definition of purpose, it should then follow that business also has a common understanding, a single and agreed-upon definition of the term "profit," and hence a uniform method of measurement and evaluation of performance in terms of profitability. If, in fact, the multiple paths of the business enterprise do lead to a common goal of profit, logic alone would suggest that the target not only be clearly visible but that an acceptable norm in terms of *profit standards* be mutually agreed upon, that success or failure be clearly defined in measurable terms.

Logic, however, which has apparently served to point

all business toward a common goal, seems to be discarded at this point in favor of a multitude of opinions and measurements—a multitude of opinion as to what profit really is, and an equally wide range of choice in the measurement of accomplishment. Profit appears to have not one measurable definition, but many. The profit goal, apparently, is not a single, visible target, but a choice of several targets to be selected at random, depending on the subjective judgment of management. The profit motive so wholeheartedly endorsed by business in general not only lacks direction but suffers from a simple lack of both definition and purpose.

Consequently, the role of profits in business is the most talked about and probably the least understood of all aspects of business management. Hotly defended in principle when threatened by controls and taxation, profit is vigorously described as being at the very heart of the capitalist system, a vital and completely necessary ingredient for continued growth and economic well-being. In practice, however, profit is poorly understood and loosely measured, resulting in a wide proliferation of opinion as to what constitutes profit, why it should be earned, and particularly how it should be measured. The problem is widespread.

In failing to heed its own rhetoric in defense of the profit system, business management has given rise to a confused body of public opinion which tends to view the whole concept of profit as either totally unnecessary or as socially undesirable. Profits are blamed for rising costs and unemployment, are often the root cause of strikes and excessive wage demands, and are frequently regarded as the result of favored tax treatment extended to business at the expense of the individual. This latter image is, in fact, considerably enhanced by the very wording of tax regulations concerning "excess profits" and "undistributed profits," words that in themselves suggest an undue enrichment or undesirable gain on the part of business. Profit "controls" are advocated as a means of holding down inflation, or price controls are imposed to keep profits in line. Business is urged to down-grade the profit motive, to redirect its efforts into the so-called larger areas of social responsibility, to subordinate profit goals for environmental objectives, to place the needs of the community ahead of the demand for earnings.

Lacking a clear understanding or common concept of the actual role of profit in business, management itself becomes a part of that same confused body of opinion, frequently failing to differentiate between accomplishment and reward, between cause and effect. In succumbing to such popular demands, moreover, it is dealing with goals and objectives which are neither overly idealistic nor in any way undesirable in themselves. The trouble is that it is simply dealing with them in exactly the wrong order, establishing a sequence of objectives that cannot be attained without a complete reversal of the priorities. It is, in short, seeking goals that cannot be met without the foundation of profit, and at the same time failing to make the need for profit understood in even the simplest of terms.

The fault, moreover, does not lie with the general public attitude toward profit, nor does it originate with government controls and taxation. The fault lies directly with business management itself, with those who should be among the first not only fully to comprehend the role of profits in a free society, but among the first to give them a clear definition of meaning and substance. The failure of management to meet this challenge is evidenced not by the relatively few but by the vast majority of business operations and financial reports. It is evidenced in both the form and content of the typical financial statement, and most particularly in the manner in which profits are described. It appears in a variety of charts and graphs and summaries which purport to show a path of continued progress toward a goal that is neither defined nor identified. It is reflected in claims of "profit" when in fact no profit exists, is evident in written reports that continue to demonstrate the widespread lack of understanding of the fundamental role of profits in business.

The fault may well be more inadvertent than intentional, with management's thinking in all likelihood strongly conditioned by the confines of bookkeeping practice and accounting procedure, a language more dedicated to form than to substance and more concerned with routine than with broad statements of purpose. With the continued use of accounting terminology and accounting statements as the vehicle for profit measurement, management has gradually adopted the technician's view of profit as a "realized increase in quantity or value," or as "gains in value measured in money terms," to quote from two definitions found in early accounting literature. These limited concepts of profit have had a profound impact on business in the reporting of past financial results, in the setting of future financial objectives, and in the multitude of operating decisions made to further such objectives.

The thought process is conditioned not only by the various measurements of profit which the accounting reports have introduced, but more importantly by the implied definition of profit as a "remainder value" at the bottom of the operating statement, which suggests that "being in the black" at this point of measurement equates with a statement of profitability. Since uniform accounting practice identifies profit with this "bottom line" figure, it is perhaps a natural assumption that the primary financial goal of any business should be black ink rather than red ink at the bottom of the statement, and that black ink and profit are therefore synonymous in that

[5]

the level of profitability of the enterprise can be measured by the amount of black ink required to report the "profit." Since no definitive target for effective profit measurement is even proposed by the accounting presentation, the question of how much profits ought to be is seldom raised.

The answer to such a question is not found in arbitrary controls imposed on the price/cost structure or in the language of tax regulations, which at times appear to be in direct opposition to the very concept of profit itself. Nor is it found in the well-intentioned if confused attempts to relegate the role of profit to a purely secondary position in the management of business. The answer lies in a far more fundamental understanding and definition of the meaning of profit, which carries with it a very basic premise: *Profit is the compensation accruing to the entrepreneur for the assumption of risk.*

Seen in this light, profit can be viewed as neither an increase in quantity nor a gain in money value, but rather as a *requirement* of normal business operations. It can be put into proper perspective as a basic obligation to be met, a price to be paid if the business itself is to continue and prosper. Profit goals and profit measurements can be given *qualitative* as well as quantitative values, with profit objectives and accomplishments stated in terms of specific *need*—a need which must be met before any of the social or environmental benefits expected of business can be realized.

To accomplish this awareness and to deal both logically and effectively with the management of profit, management will have to redefine much of its present terminology and to discard many of its former concepts of the financial elements it is dealing with. To most managers, for example, the terms "cost" and "expense" refer solely to the operating charges incurred for the three basic elements of materials, labor, and overhead involved in the typical business operation, charges which are duly recorded on the books of account and then reflected in meticulous detail on the subsequent accounting statements. Having thus defined the cost of doing business as the sum total of completed transactions charged against income for the period, the accounting concept further defines "profit" as the excess of income over recorded cost, the precise difference measured from the casting up of the operating accounts as shown on the Trial Balance.

The management view of profit is thus limited to the tunnel vision afforded by the accounting process, a process which confines itself to a recording of the monetary value of income versus outgo, or words to that effect. The accounting statement says, in essence, "Here is what has happened up to this point. Here is a report of the excess of credits over debits to the operating accounts for the period just ended. For lack of a better word, the difference is referred to as 'profit.'" In reality, the accounting presentation makes no attempt to go beyond this point, makes no assumption of a qualitative value in its reported measurement of profit. Nor was it ever designed to do so, to offer more than a certain limited set of facts as a point of departure for management evaluation and control. The fact that so many managers regard the typical financial statement not as a beginning point but as an end point of measurement cannot be blamed on the accounting process itself, but reflects instead the failure of management to understand the nature of the financial elements it must manage.

Every manager, for example, would readily agree that no "profit" can be said to exist until the business has first recovered its costs, and would probably also regard such a statement as being too obvious to be worthy of discussion. He would not, for equally obvious reasons, accept a financial report of profit which omitted the basic cost of raw materials consumed in production, nor a report which showed a "profit" without the proper charges for major elements of operating overhead. On the other hand, he is quite willing to accept—and indeed has been conditioned to accept—statements of reported "profit" which repeatedly omit a major element of the cost of doing business. He is thus typically unaware of the fact that there are not three but four major cost elements to be recovered in the average business, and that to be truly profitable a company must recover *all* of its costs, including the fourth element, the cost of capital employed.

The Cost of Capital

The concept that capital has a cost and that the cost of capital must be recovered is by no means new. It has been well propounded in theory and ably developed in financial literature, but somehow remains either academic or largely theoretical to the great majority of business managers. In retrospect, it apparently takes on such theoretical qualities for two basic reasons. First, the accounting procedures which govern the content of most financial reporting to management do not reflect the cost of total capital employed anywhere in the operating statement. And coupled with such "evidence" that the manager is thus not accountable for the cost of capital is the second basic consideration that nothing apparently happens—at least over the short term—if this "theoretical cost" is thus completely ignored. With these two counts against it, it is at least understandable why the subject is regarded by so many as being of little more than statistical interest.

It is, of course, far from being a theoretical or statistical element of cost in spite of the contrary implications suggested by accounting practice and despite the lack of measurable penalties over the short term. For while these factors have undoubtedly served to obscure the value of the measurement, they also serve to place an even greater emphasis on the need on the part of management to understand the basic demand which the cost of capital places on operating results.

Capital is a commodity, and like any other commodity it has a price. Just as the costs of materials, labor, and services are finally determined by the law of supply and demand, so is the price to be paid for the use of capital determined by the risk/reward ratios prevailing in the marketplace. Capital is supplied by the investor, and unlike other commodities used in business it does not have a common cost for all buyers in like quantities. Nor, despite many opinions to the contrary, can the overall cost effectively be reduced by negotiating for various sources of supply. The cost of capital used in business is not determined by its source, that is, where the capital comes from, but on how it is used. It is a unique commodity, one which will eventually go where it is treated best, a commodity which carries with it a cost determined by expectation rather than by contract. It is invested or put to work by the investor in those opportunities which offer the best expectation of return commensurate with the risk of the undertaking. It is supplied on a calculated basis, a basis which weighs both the opportunities and the attendant risks in alternate choices of investment and which then carefully follows the process of evaluating risk against expected return. It is a market based on the expectation of performance, a market which will readily assume risk but which also readily demands a suitable rate of return.

The market for capital measures its compensation for risk in terms of earnings, and is found to have a rather precise definition of the terms "earnings" and "profits," a specific measurement of exactly how much the profits should be. It is not content with "black ink" or with other partial measurements of reported profit, but looks to the adequacy of profits as the price to be paid for the use of capital supplied, a rate of return which justifies the level of risk assumed. It equates the cost of capital with a *profit requirement*, a demand by the investor which must ultimately be met by management if it is to maintain the ability to attract new capital, or even to keep the capital it has already acquired.

Since the investor supplies the capital used in business, he also supplies his own evaluation of risk, and with it the rate of return expected. It is thus the investor, not the management of the company, who determines the present cost of capital. Management, in turn, will ultimately affect the *future* cost of capital for the business through its own performance, a performance based largely on its ability to meet the expectation of earnings. It can do this successfully only if it fully understands the nature of the risk/return relationship and places the profit requirement in perspective as a specific target to be attained, a cost of doing business which must be paid.

To accomplish this effectively, to be able to define specific goals and objectives for the rate of profit required, management must develop an awareness and understanding of the evaluation of risk as seen through the eyes of the investor. It starts with the obvious premise that *all* investment entails risk, and that risk itself is therefore a relative measure varying only in degree as between different investment opportunities. It next follows that an overall evaluation of risk is a *composite* evaluation of many factors, a composite assumption of probability that certain events will or will not occur over a period of time. It contains a variety of elements. The risk of total loss is certainly considered; if found too high, it would obviously outweigh or override all other probabilities. The risk of total loss would, for example, be presumed to be the greatest single element of risk in evaluating new ventures or new technology, areas where experience is totally lacking and where the possibility of total failure becomes a distinct reality. In the more ordinary course of business, however, the risk of total loss tends to diminish in probability and is supplanted by questions of how well or how poorly the business may be managed and operated over a period of time. The question of risk then centers around the degree of probability for success —in other words, the chances that the enterprise can produce earnings which will represent an adequate rate of return for the investor.

In the overall evaluation of risk, many factors come under review. If the business has already been in operation for a period of time, the record of earnings already achieved is clearly given considerable weight, as well as an appraisal of how well past performance can be repeated or improved upon in the future. Behind this basic premise, the question of risk includes an opinion of the industry involved, its future in the economy, the share of market or position in industry of the company in question, the competence of management, the future of new product development or of technological obsolescence, the record of sales growth, and perhaps dozens of other factors depending upon the particular investment opportunity under review. The degree of risk given to each of these elements or the weighting given to each probability in this process is obviously not available to management in any exact detail, and indeed is seldom computed as a mathematical exercise by the investor himself. In other words, the overall evaluation of risk and the resulting cost of capital to the business can never be computed as a precise figure or as an exact calculation. It must be used as an estimate, as an order of magnitude appraisal, as a guide to management planning and control. Its importance, however, is by no means diminished by the lack of precise measurement. This factor simply places a greater burden on management: first to understand the nature of the profit requirement, and second to select a profit measurement which will properly reflect attainment of the profit goal.

Profit goals for management cannot be attained if they are to remain as abstract concepts. They need a measurement which will contain both a quantitative and a qualitative evaluation of results, a composite measure which will define not only the level of profit required but also the need for the rate of attainment itself. Failure to do so will lead to partial measurements and incomplete goals, to financial objectives which offer the illusion of profit while masking the gradual erosion of earning power. Failure to do so will inevitably lead to a series of management decisions that will serve to enhance the apparent results at the expense of the ultimate need.

Management, in short, has a need to discard its accounting definitions of profit and to look upon it as the payment due on capital invested at risk. It is a requirement which management must face, if for no other reason than the fact that those who supply the capital have already done so.

one

Return on invested capital

$\mathcal{M}$ANY MANAGERS will subscribe to the "return on investment" concept of profit measurement without giving serious thought as to what is meant by the word "return" or what is included in the definition of the term "investment." But while acceptance of the concept itself can be considered a major step in the direction of a valid measurement of profit, it needs specific definition if it is to be used as a guide to operating decisions and as a measurement of financial results.

There are, in fact, several "return on investment"

types of financial measurements commonly used in business, but only one which is complete in every respect,
and only one which can be said to measure the total
earning power of the business. This is generally described
as the *Return on Invested Capital* measurement, which
not only fully defines "return" as the total stream of
earnings from operations, but which also fully defines
"investment" as the total capital employed in the business. To a large extent, it has been the measurement of the
financial analyst rather than the operating tool of management, the final appraisal of corporate profitability rather
than the interim measurement of profit performance. It
is, however, rapidly becoming the accepted standard of
management performance in many of the leading financial
publications and is gaining wide acceptance in reports
which analyze and rank the largest corporations in the
country on the basis of their relative profitability rather
than on size alone.

In further defining profitability as the rate of return
on invested capital, one publication has stated quite flatly
that it is the most meaningful measure of any company's
success. With management thus measured by this standard
in full public view, it will sooner or later respond, as indeed many alert managements have already done, by
adopting the same measurement for its own use, by
establishing financial objectives and measurements which
conform to this evaluation of performance. The transition gradually taking place in this direction would then
seem to offer some evidence that the profit measure main-
tains economic validity if and only if the return is calculated as a true overall economic rate of return for the
business.

The use of return on invested capital as the only valid
measure of economic profit has been slow to gain acceptance in the past for several reasons. First and foremost is

perhaps the basic lack of understanding on the part of management as to what is involved, how it is measured, and particularly what impact it has on the entire decision-making process. Behind this rather fundamental barrier, management has been, and still is, at a distinct disadvantage in trying to develop the measurement as a readily adaptable operating tool, for the simple reason that the values used in the determination of the rate of return on invested capital are seldom available from the typical accounting presentation of the usual financial statements. With minor exceptions, *neither the total earnings of the business nor a composite statement of the total capital employed to produce the earnings is reported directly by the accounting process*, a lack of definitive reporting that can be presumed to make use of the measurement a difficult task at best. The easier path, by far, has been to link up the several segments of the financial information in the manner in which they are presented in the accounting statement, and to measure "profit" in terms of the net dollars reported, as a percent of sales volume or as a rate of return either on the total assets or on the equity portion of the total capital, values which are easily identified and normally reported as separate elements directly on the financial statements. It is certainly a natural assumption that if the financial elements of the business are normally displayed and reported in this fashion, the form of the report must have a purpose and that a useful measurement should result in the bringing together of the apparent results. What is not apparent, and indeed what is almost completely obscured by the accounting presentation, is the fact referred to in the Introduction that such reports are not designed to provide a final measurement of results but to serve as no more than a point of departure for further analysis and evaluation.

While the measurement of return on invested capital is

thus not readily determined from the typical financial report, and is therefore a somewhat more difficult tool to develop for the use of operating management, it is used as the leading indicator of the profitability and economic earning power of a business for one very significant reason. *It is the only financial measurement available which can be described as a total measurement,* one which omits nothing in the financial evaluation of results. This is not to suggest that it is by any means the only measurement or the only piece of information needed to evaluate the total strength of a business, or that in itself it can serve to indicate the future course or probable trend the business may take.

A complete evaluation of any business would necessarily require much more in the way of additional intelligence, much more in the way of additional information concerning sales growth, the backlog of business on hand, the share of market, production costs and production rates, the utilization of capacity, the use of specific assets employed, and many more related bits of operating detail. Such additional information, however, would also be needed in support of any single measurement of profit used and thus would apply equally to all of them, leaving the validity of the profit evaluation alone to be tested simply on its own merits. This, then, simplifies the task of analyzing the profit measurement in terms of what it includes—or, in many cases, in what it omits—in the financial sense only. As has been stated, the Return on Invested Capital measurement provides a complete evaluation on both sides of the equation, complete as to total earnings and complete as to total capital investment. Since it is the only profit measurement to do so, the full meaning of both *earnings* and *invested capital* must be explored in some detail before the measurement can be fully defined or usefully put to work.

Invested Capital

As used in this measurement, the term "invested capital" is sometimes referred to as the total capital employed, and includes all of the capital used in the business, regardless of its source. Following the premise that it is not where the capital comes from but the risk at which it is put to use in the business which will determine its ultimate cost, capital is thus treated as a single entity, a common pool of resources which supports the entire operation of the enterprise. At this point of measurement, no distinction is made between the borrowed funds represented by debt capital and the ownership funds represented by the equity capital, since the funds themselves are commingled or combined into a common pool. The total risk is thus likewise commingled and total capital is thus a single unit having a composite requirement as to earnings. Following this reasoning, the relationship between the two sources of capital—the debt and the equity—is not disregarded but (as will be seen later) is used in turn to measure the adequacy of the earnings rate itself.

In those instances where the current value of the total capital employed in the business can be measured directly from the Balance Sheet, there are two methods by which the total invested capital can be determined—two methods because the books have been "balanced" by the process of double-entry bookkeeping which records equal values on both sides of each transaction entered in the books of account. The first method, and usually the easier, is to take the Total *Assets* as listed on the Balance Sheet and subtract from this total *the sum of all the noninterest-bearing debt.* The resulting net figure will represent the Total Invested Capital or the total capital employed at common risk whose cost must be paid for in an adequate rate of earnings. The second method will provide the same

[17]

answer, but is often a bit more difficult to compute on the more complex statements of the larger companies. This involves the adding together of *all the elements of interest-bearing debt* and *all the elements of equity capital*. Since the books are assumed to be in balance, the answer will be the same by either method, but the second approach often requires a more exact knowledge of accounting terminology in order to be able to identify the various elements of the capital structure.

Debt Capital

Of the two possible sources of capital, debt and equity, debt capital is probably the easier to identify in the typical accounting report. It may be variously described in such segments as mortgage notes, notes payable, bonds, and debentures, or in various forms of subordinated debt. It will frequently be divided into two general categories or groups which will identify the debt as either *short-term* or *long-term*, depending on the due dates for the various classes of obligations. Listed under Current Liabilities will be all of the debt falling due within the ensuing 12 months (the short-term debt), with the remainder listed under the heading of long-term debt or long-term liabilities. Regardless of how it is described, however, or where it may be listed on the Balance Sheet, the total debt capital employed in the business will be distinguished by one common characteristic: *It will be interest-bearing.* As such, it can be considered as *negotiated debt*, or debt capital, which management has raised at various times in lieu of seeking new equity capital and for which it has negotiated not only the interest rate and the dates for the eventual repayment of principal, but the collateral given as security, together with the various debt restrictions normally imposed as a condition of the loan. It is clearly *risk* capital to be used in the general conduct of the business, a portion of the total capital employed which must be paid for through earnings. It is, in other words, the *character of the debt* and not the due date which identifies it as part of the total capital of the company.

In contrast to the interest-bearing debt, debt which is negotiated as an addition to the capital structure, the noninterest-bearing debt is not a part of the invested capital and is therefore excluded from the investment base on which the earnings are computed. Typically referred to as "operating debt," it is incurred not as additional capital but simply as a by-product of operations, a reflection of the normal terms of credit granted in the ordinary course of business. The operating, or noninterest-bearing debt, is usually identified under the heading of Current Liabilities in such accounts as Accounts Payable, Accrued Expenses, Accrued Taxes, and the like, statements of amounts due in the near term for assets which have not yet been paid for or which represent the temporary use of the supplier's capital. Operating debt of this nature is not included in the calculation of invested capital for the simple reasons that *it carries with it no earnings requirement*, and that it is not a part of the risk capital whose use must be justified in the form of an adequate rate of return to the investor. It is exempted because it represents assets *whose use is already being paid for in a different fashion*—in the price of goods and services received. In other words, the supplier who furnishes raw materials on open credit with terms of "30 days net" is supplying an asset to be used by the company which is actually supported by the supplier's capital for 30 days. It is not "free capital" in any sense of the word because the price charged for the materials will—if properly computed—already include the use of the supplier's money for the 30-day period of credit. Since it is thus already paid for in the acquisition cost of the asset, inclusion of this value in the investment base against which earnings are to be measured would result in a double charge, which would seriously distort the use of the profit measurement.

Equity Capital

The other source of capital—the ownership funds represented by the equity investment in the business—is often more difficult to determine because of accounting distinctions afforded to various segments of the equity. Most easily recognizable is the section of the Balance Sheet identified as Net Worth, a term which should be synonymous with equity investment but which, again, is more frequently limited to the more precise demands of accounting practice. Under the heading of Net Worth will usually be found the value at which the common and preferred stock of the corporation is carried on the books, a value representing not the current market but the original net proceeds received by the company upon issuance of the shares. Added to this will be the Retained Earnings or earned surplus representing the accumulation of past earnings which have accrued to the benefit of the equity investor but which have been held back at the discretion of management to be used for future growth instead of being returned in the form of current dividends. Added to these accounts may be various elements described as capital surplus, amounts of capital arising from transactions involving acquisitions and mergers or from a recapitalization in some prior period. Individually they describe how the net worth of the company came into being, but collectively they represent the bulk of the total equity capital employed.

The difficulty in determining the entire total of the

equity capital of a business, however, usually lies outside the so-called net worth section of the Balance Sheet and has to do with the listing of many independent accounts shown separately on the statement, accounts which do not readily identify themselves by description alone and which often take some intimate knowledge of accounting nomenclature to place correctly in the capital structure. Typical among this latter group would be values ascribed to Deferred Income Taxes, to Reserves for Contingencies, Deposits on Uncompleted Contracts, and the like. Since even the accountants themselves do not always agree on either the form or the substance of such accounts, the proper identification as between debt capital and equity capital can be a difficult one. For this reason alone the method of determining invested capital as the net difference between total assets and total operating debt is by far the simpler, even though it lacks the ability to differentiate between debt and equity or to measure the debt/equity ratio of the total capital employed.

By either approach, however, the determination of invested capital for purposes of measuring the net rate of return should not be made as of a single point in time. Earnings for the year, for example, are not produced solely by the level of capital employed at the beginning of the year, nor are they the result of the capital balance at the close of the year, a level which is frequently higher in the average business. Capital tends to accumulate and grow over a period of time, but may be either sharply increased or decreased during the year, depending on the circumstances surrounding the business or simply as a result of arbitrary decisions taken by management with respect to the use of debt or equity, or both. It is, then, neither the beginning, the ending, or even the midpoint level of capital employed that serves as the basis for measurement, but rather the *average* investment in capital which produced the earnings for the period under review. On a practical basis, a useful average can generally be computed as the weighted average of monthly levels of capital employed, a technique which overcomes the seasonal effect of the use of borrowed capital in many lines of business as well as the impact of increasing amounts of equity capital built up through the accumulation of retained earnings over a period of time.

As has already been noted, the separation of total invested capital into the primary categories of debt and equity constitutes an important measurement of both total risk as well as the adequacy of the earnings reported. Equity capital provides the base upon which the *borrowing capacity* of a company can be measured, and the extent to which such borrowing capacity has been used—or at times misused—will also serve to determine the probable change in total risk and thus the need for a different level of earnings. While all capital can be considered as risk capital employed in a business, the varying degrees of risk between the debt and equity capital segments become subordinate measurements which have a qualitative effect on the use of the Return on Invested Capital measurement of profit. The impact of excessive debt, in particular, is best demonstrated in situations where the capital is said to be highly "leveraged," a subject that will be dealt with at some length in a later examination of the use of Return on Equity and its relationship to the Return on Capital concept.

The Measurement of Total Earnings

For a relatively few companies—those having no negotiated interest-bearing debt—the total equity capital and the total invested capital employed in the business will be one and the same. For these same few companies—

assuming again that the book value of capital is representative of the total current value of the capital employed—the accounted net profit after taxes or figure for net book earnings will also represent the total earnings on total capital. In the great majority of corporate financial reports, however, the accounted or net book earnings figure cannot be related to total capital employed and in fact is often highly misleading with respect to relative profitability. Since varying amounts of debt capital will be found in the reports of most companies, the accounted net earnings figure is no more than a hybrid report, a figure representing *what is left over after a portion of the cost of capital has been paid for*. It is, in other words, an earnings figure from which the interest cost on the debt capital has already been deducted, and represents only the remainder of the earnings accruing to the equity ownership of the business. Use of such an earnings figure in computing the rate of return on invested capital would obviously result in a double charge for the use of debt—once in the inclusion of debt capital in the investment base, and a second time in the inclusion of the interest expense on the same debt capital as a reduction of the accounted net earnings.

It is for this reason that the earnings figure used in the return on invested capital measurement is referred to as the *total stream of earnings from operations*, or the level of profits earned before any of the capital was paid for. To adjust back to this level, it is then necessary to *add the interest expense back* to the reported earnings to arrive at the total earnings to be measured against total capital employed. Since the rate of return is normally measured on an after-tax basis—the amount left for the investor—it is also the after-tax cost of the interest payments which must be added to the net earnings. It is perhaps at this

[23]

very point that the inadequacy of the accounting statement will become most obvious and the fact that it serves only as a point of departure for further analysis and evaluation more readily understandable.

The Calculation of Return on Invested Capital

A practical application of the concepts and principles already discussed with regard to the content of invested capital and the necessity of measuring total earnings can perhaps best be demonstrated by working out the rate of return on invested capital, using typical values in a hypothetical company. For this purpose, the financial statements of The Average Manufacturing Company are shown in the accompanying typical accounting presentations.

Exhibit A

The Average Manufacturing Company Income Statement (Years Ending December 31, 19X2 and 19X1)		
	19X2	19X1
Sales	$30,000	$26,000
Cost of Goods Sold	22,500	19,500
Gross Profit	7,500	6,500
Selling Expense	2,500	2,200
Administrative Expense	2,000	1,700
Operating Profit	3,000	2,600
Interest on Debt Capital	180	120
Profit Before Tax	2,820	2,480
Taxes on Income	1,410	1,240
Net Earnings	$ 1,410	$ 1,240

Exhibit B

The Average Manufacturing Company Balance Sheet (December 31) ASSETS			
	19X2	19X1	19X0
Current Assets			
Cash in Bank and on Hand	$ 800	$ 700	$ 600
Accounts Receivable	4,000	3,500	3,000
Inventory	9,400	5,000	4,000
Prepaid Expenses	2,500	2,100	1,900
Total Current Assets	$16,700	$11,300	$ 9,500
Fixed Assets			
Net Plant and Equipment	6,400	5,600	4,800
Total Assets	$23,100	$16,900	$14,300

LIABILITIES AND NET WORTH

	19X2	19X1	19X0
Current Liabilities			
Accounts Payable	$ 4,000	$ 900	$ 1,000
Accrued Taxes and Expenses	3,100	2,000	1,300
Total Current Liabilities	$ 7,100	$ 2,900	$ 2,300
Long-Term Debt	3,500	2,500	1,500
Net Worth			
Common Stock—1,000 Shares	10,000	10,000	10,000
Retained Earnings	2,500	1,500	500
Total Net Worth	$12,500	$11,500	$10,500
Total Liabilities and Net Worth	$23,100	$16,900	$14,300

A brief analysis of the Balance Sheet will show that the total invested capital of The Average Manufacturing Company can be readily computed by either of the two methods previously discussed.

[25]

	19X2	19X1	19X0
First Method			
Total Assets	$23,100	$16,900	$14,300
Less Operating Debt	7,100	2,900	2,300
Invested Capital	$16,000	$14,000	$12,000
Second Method			
Debt Capital	$ 3,500	$ 2,500	$ 1,500
Equity Capital	12,500	11,500	10,500
Invested Capital	$16,000	$14,000	$12,000

As a further step in the calculation, it will also be noted that the *average* capital employed during the year 19X1 was $13,000, which is the average of the opening balance of $12,000 at the end of 19X0 and the closing balance of $14,000 on December 31, 19X1. In like fashion, the average capital employed in the latest year is shown to be $15,000, values against which the total earnings of the company will be measured for each of the two years in question.

In turning to the operating statement of income for each of these two years, it will next be noted that the interest charges on debt capital have served to reduce the accounted net earnings in each year, and that the total interest cost in the second year has increased in direct proportion to the increase in the average level of debt capital employed. The calculation of total earnings on total capital can then be determined as follows:

	19X2	19X1
Accounted Net Earnings	$1,410	$1,240
Add Net Interest Cost	90	60
Total Earnings	$1,500	$1,300

In adding back the net interest cost to arrive at the total earnings from operations, it will be seen that an effective income tax rate of 50% has been assumed in

[26]

each year so that the net after-tax cost of interest expense to the company is also 50%, or one-half, of the total amount paid.

By then bringing together the computed total earnings and the calculation of average invested capital for each of the two years it will be found that the rate of return on invested capital remained constant during this period, despite higher sales and an apparent increase in reported "profit" during the second year of operations.

	19X2	19X1
Total Earnings	$ 1,500	$ 1,300
Average Invested Capital	$15,000	$13,000
Rate of Return, %	10	10

In other words, the apparent "gain" in the reported dollars of profit was no gain at all, but merely represented an increase in the level of dollar earnings commensurate with a corresponding increase in the level of capital employed. As will be seen later, however, several other measurements of "profit" applied to these same financial statements will suggest several quite different interpretations of the operating results.

The Adequacy of Profits

Alone among the various measurements of profit commonly used in business, the measurement of rate of return on invested capital provides not only a complete quantitative measurement but a *qualitative* measurement as well. It thus provides a true economic rate of return which measures the overall earning power of the business, and at the same time provides a standard by which the adequacy of the earnings themselves can be judged. For all intents and purposes, that standard can be assumed to be a 10% rate of return for the average industrial company over a reasonable period of time. It is, admittedly, a rough benchmark that is by no means precise enough for the setting of financial goals and objectives for any one individual company, nor is it precise enough for testing the adequacy of earnings for any single industry. On the other hand, it is an average which is well documented in the experience of a broad segment of industry as an accepted standard rate of return. As such, *it provides the only benchmark or valid means of comparison available on any measurement of profit.*

The 10% rate of return on invested capital is well documented as the average rate of return attained by the six or seven hundred largest corporations in the country over a period of years, an average which sets a standard in the sense that every other business can be presumed to be competing for capital at no less than a 10% rate of return to the investor. And since, like any average, it also means that approximately one-half of the largest companies being measured were earning a higher rate of return while the other half were earning less than 10%, it also suggests that the average of a 10% return represents a *minimum* acceptable rate as compensation for the risk at which the capital has been employed.

It also provides a starting point from which a more precise measurement of the cost of capital—that is, what the rate of return ought to be—can be developed for any single business. As a first step, the overall average rates of return are also measured and published by industry groupings, rates which will serve to bring the measurement closer to a useful standard for the *type* of business being considered. Second, the process can next be refined by an examination of the published reports of major competitors within a given industry, a step which will again narrow down the range of the average rate of return provided by competitive capital. And last, a review of the company's own record of earnings over the past several years will serve to establish the relative level that management should seek in setting its own objectives for financial performance. In thus establishing a specific rate of return on capital as the total earnings requirement of the business, it is of no practical consequence that the figure itself must be derived as no more than a reasonable approximation of the cost of capital. Business is already accustomed to dealing with reasonable approximations, particularly in the case of depreciation charges made against operating income, and it is of far greater importance that an order of magnitude measurement be made than that it be omitted for lack of precision.

Once adopted, the measurement of return on invested capital will serve management well and will become the final yardstick against which many new and more fruitful decisions will be made. Achievement of an adequate rate of return on capital will automatically insure that all other possible measurements of profitability will also reach proper levels. Therefore, decisions which might have been made to enhance simply the return on sales or the return on equity will now be put into proper perspective and balanced against the total effect on the economic earnings of the business. Decisions which might have been taken with the objective of simply increasing the earnings per share will also now be examined to insure that apparent gains in terms of one measurement are not made at the expense of an actual loss of capital on the other. And while the full impact of the effect such management decisions can have on the final results of the business must necessarily await a more detailed examination of the use of other profit measurements to be discussed in the following chapters, the concept of the Return on Capital measurement marks it as the only *complete* measurement of profitability available in business. It stands as a final statement of total earnings in which nothing is left out, a statement which cannot be used to report apparent

[29]

"profits" while masking the gradual erosion of earning power.

In the final analysis, the measurement will be put to use by those managements who are truly concerned with the long-range success and fundamental strength of the enterprise they have been hired to manage. And for the very reason that it does serve as both a guide and an indicator of long-term stability and economic growth, it will also be avoided by those managements more concerned with the short-term effects that the more manipulative types of profit reporting can at times produce with respect to the current market price of corporate shares and the consequent attractiveness of executive stock options.

two

Return on assets

A SECOND MEASUREMENT OF PROFIT, and one more
frequently used by management, is the evaluation
of profit as a percentage rate of return on the total
assets of the business. It follows the Return on Investment concept of financial reporting and at the
same time supplies a finite definition of the investment base as being the sum total of all of the assets
recorded on the Balance Sheet. Since the total assets
of a business are usually easier to identify than the
figure for total invested capital, the measurement
would seem to have the virtue of being more di-

rectly measurable and more readily understandable to the average manager. It would also appear, by its very definition, to be an evaluation of earnings based on the total resources employed by the business. For this reason it is often regarded as a financial measurement roughly comparable to return on invested capital, an overall measurement of the economic earning power of the business. In this respect it is thought to measure the effectiveness of management in putting the assets of the business to work, a measurement which judges overall profit performance as opposed to reports which present only partial results on segmented portions of the business activity. And to a great extent the assumptions implied by the Return on Assets evaluation are indeed valid.

Its greatest claim to validity lies in the fact that it does include the use of debt capital in the investment base, and to this extent it follows the concept laid down for the measurement of return on invested capital; that is, it is not where the resources come from but how they are put to work that determines the true profitability of the enterprise. Since the total assets of a business necessarily include the combined use of both debt and equity capital as a common pool or common resource to be put to work, the measurement of profit as a rate of return on total assets automatically includes the use of negotiated interest-bearing debt and avoids any tendency to overstate the reported results through the use of leverage or changes in the debt/equity ratio of the capital structure. And while this single aspect of the measurement is indeed of fundamental importance, it is the only redeeming feature or strong point in its favor. For while it is perhaps a close second to the Return on Invested Capital measurement in terms of being a relatively valid evaluation of profit and is indeed far superior to many other measurements in common use, it nevertheless has several inherent weaknesses that make it less than useful as an overall guide to profit performance or profit objectives.

These weaknesses lie in the fact that the Return on Assets measurement typically *overstates the investment and understates the earnings,* weaknesses which can seriously distort the assessment of profitability for the average company. The investment is typically overstated for the average business due to the fact that the measurement combines all assets into a single total without regard to their source and without regard to basic differences in the cost of asset management. Just as invested capital is recognized as having a cost in terms of a level of earnings commensurate with the risk, so do the total assets of a business have a cost in terms of profit performance. The economic cost of the total assets employed, however, is not a single entity as it is for invested capital and is, in fact, made up of two entirely separate types of cost which warrant separate measurements.

The total assets of the average business are supplied by two fundamentally different sources, sources which will vary in magnitude from time to time and which have widely disparate demands as to economic cost. The primary source of assets used in business, the one which will typically account for some 80% of the total assets employed, is the invested capital of the company, the aggregate of the interest-bearing debt and the equity funds already described. This source of funds must indeed be paid for, or justify its economic level of cost, in the adequacy of the total earnings of the business. As noted previously, however, the other roughly 20% of the total assets employed are not furnished by the invested capital but by trade creditors who supply a continuing stream of assets to the company on terms of open credit. The extent to which assets are furnished from this direction can normally be measured directly as the sum of the *current operating debt* or noninterest-bearing obligations evidenced by such items as accounts payable, accrued payroll, and accrued taxes and expenses. As also previously described, the cost for the use of these assets is already included in the price of goods and services received, a cost calculated in the selling price to cover the use of the supplier's money for the term of credit extended. To include these assets in the total investment base against which earnings are to be measured is thus quite obviously an overstatement of investment, a doubling up of the charge to be levied against a rather sizable portion of the total assets employed.

This overstatement of investment is then further compounded by a typical understatement of earnings in the use of the Return on Assets measurement of profit. When used in business, the rate of return on assets not only uses the base of total assets just described, *but also normally relates this base to the accounted or net book earnings* as shown on the operating statement. This, in turn, results in a double charge for the use of the interest-bearing debt capital: once, since it is included in the measurement of total assets, and then once again, since the accounted net earnings have already been reduced by the total amount of interest paid on the same debt capital. When viewed in this light, it will be seen that the profit measurement of return on assets can be highly misleading, particularly when used as a standard of comparison over a period of time.

In practice, it can take on a certain degree of *relative value* under some rather limited conditions. For those companies where no debt capital is employed, where 100% of the invested capital of the business is supplied by equity funds, the objection to the understatement of earnings is removed. If it can then also be found that the average operating debt for the trade payables is relatively constant in relation to the total assets employed in the business, the measurement of return on assets—while not maintaining economic validity—will at least provide a consistent reading in terms of trend analysis. As a final step, if this same business were then operated completely on a cash basis and had no payables whatsoever, the measurement would then become a completely valid evaluation of earnings. It should be noted that under such conditions the two measurements—Return on Invested Capital and Return on Assets—would coincide and become one and the same. Total assets and total capital would then be identical, and accounted earnings and total earnings would likewise have no difference in meaning or measurement. Such situations, however, are indeed a rarity in business and would scarcely be given much serious weighting in the final choice of profit measurement.

The weaknesses thus ascribed to the Return on Assets measurement of profit, together with a direct comparison of the use of return on invested capital, can perhaps best be shown by reference to some fairly typical financial reports which have already been set forth for The Average Manufacturing Company in Chapter 1. It will be recalled that the measurement of return on invested capital for this company showed a constant level of a 10% attainment for each of the two years being measured, once the total earnings were properly weighed against the average capital employed. Using the same financial statements again, the Return on Assets measurement would be developed as shown in the following tabulation.

	19X2	19X1	19X0
A. Determination of Average Assets			
Year Ending December 31			
Total Assets	$23,100	$16,900	$14,300
Average Assets Employed	20,000	15,600	
B. Determination of Net Earnings			
Net Accounted Earnings	1,410	1,240	

	19X2	19X1	19X0
C. Determination of Profit Measurement			
Net Earnings	1,410	1,240	
Average Assets	$20,000	$15,600	
D. Return on Assets, %	7.1	8.0	

Based on this evaluation, the earnings for the two years are apparently no longer constant as in the first measurement, but have fallen off some 11% from a net return of 8.0% in the first year to only 7.1% in the second. As viewed by the investor, the measurement could then suggest a serious downtrend in earnings which might appear to jeopardize the future stock market value of the shares. And as viewed by management, performance has apparently slipped, and corrective action must be taken— in all probability in the direction of "getting the inventories back in line." Both assumptions would, of course, be completely unwarranted even though the profit measurement used would seem to point clearly to such conclusions.

A more detailed analysis of the results would quickly show that the increase in total assets in the second year had been accompanied by a corresponding level of increase in the amount of current operating debt; quite possibly an alert purchasing management had simply succeeded in negotiating extended terms for the acquisition of more inventory. If so, then the company had quite likely moved to a more favorable position, one in which it could carry more inventory investment at no increase in acquisition cost—a position which might shed a somewhat different light on the "problem" of the level of inventory. In similar fashion, the investor might also view this move as one which could conceivably enhance the company's ability to handle more volume at a greater profit, an analysis which might have a decidedly opposite effect on the future price/earnings ratio of the shares in the market. Such further analysis, however, is seldom forthcoming, since both the management and the investor could be assumed to be guided by the appearance of results and tend to accept the measurement of profit in the manner in which it was reported.

The measurement of profit as a net rate of return on assets is thus seen as less than ideal for evaluating the overall results of the business, a measurement which presents neither a true economic picture of profit nor a useful assessment of trends under normal operating conditions. The concept, however, should not be rejected out of hand as completely unworkable, since it has a somewhat unique value if the relationship of profit to assets is properly defined and clearly put into perspective.

Invested capital per se is in fact managed only for the company as a whole, and then by only a relatively few individuals at the very top level of the management structure. The success of capital management, in turn, must rest with its delegation to several subordinate levels of management if the corporate goals and objectives are to be achieved; that is, delegated in fact to managers who do not manage capital at all *but who manage simply a portion of the total capital of the company in the form of assets.* Most managers, then, manage assets instead of capital, and some measure of profit performance related to the use of assets is quite clearly needed if delegated authority and responsibility are to be evaluated in terms of overall objectives. This need is most clearly evident at the profit center level within a company, whether it be an operating division, a branch location, or the management of a single major product or product line. In each case, the operating management is responsible not only for a major share of the total income, cost, and accounted

[37]

profit of the company but also for the direct use of perhaps a major share of the company's total capital.

Many financial reports will recognize the need to identify the operating side of these activities in terms of accounted profit and will usually present some analysis or breakdown of the total results from operations in a series of divisional or product line statements. Since the concept of profit itself, however, is not too often clearly understood or defined at the top of the company, the divisional or profit center reports are frequently no more than an expanded misapplication of the profit measurement—a distortion of results which often compounds the many inherent weaknesses found in the corporate measurement itself. The most common approach is perhaps the one of thinking of profit in accounting terms as the net difference between income and recorded operating cost for the period. This same concept of profit is then carried over to the divisional reports in which an evaluation is also made in terms of accounted operating profit, quite often after making an allocation of arbitrary charges for various segments of common operating overhead. Such reports then give the appearance of carrying a proper share of "full cost" so that the sum of the reported "profit" results for each activity can be crossfooted to the exact total reported for the company as a whole. A typical financial report presented along these lines, for example, might show *apparent* results for a company with three separate operating divisions (see Table 1).

Based on the information reported, management might then be expected to draw the following conclusions:

1. Division B is clearly the most profitable of the three divisions with an operating profit of $73,500 for the year —a figure which accounts for nearly 150% of the total

Table 1

	Division A	Division B	Division C	Total
Units Sold	50,000	30,000	20,000	100,000
Price, $	8.00	15.00	7.50	10.00
Net Sales, $	400,000	450,000	150,000	1,000,000
Cost of Sales, $	330,000	270,000	100,000	700,000
Gross Profit, $	70,000	180,000	50,000	300,000
Percent to Sales*	17.5	40.0	33.3	30.0
Selling Expense, $	60,000	67,500	22,500	150,000
Administrative Expense, $	47,000	39,000	14,000	100,000
Total	$107,000	$106,500	$36,500	$250,000
Pretax Profit	$(37,000)	$ 73,500	$13,500	$ 50,000
Income Taxes				25,000
Net Earnings				$ 25,000

results for the company on only 45% of the total volume. Operations of this division should apparently be expanded to their full potential—if necessary, at the expense of the activities of Divisions A and C.

2. Division C is likewise in a relatively good position, having earned some 27% of the total company profit on only 15% of the total sales volume. However, since the gross profit rate is only 33.3% as compared with 40.0% in Division B, it would appear obvious that higher volume here would not pay off as readily in terms of increased profits.

3. Division A, on the other hand, is apparently a major problem, having shown a $37,000 loss for the year on 40% of the total volume of business. Since both the selling price and the unit cost of production are virtually in line with expectations, little hope is held out for the future of this operation which also shows a gross profit of only 17.5% on sales. In summary, the reported results

[39]

indicate that plans should be drawn up to close down the division during the coming year.

Several things, however, are basically wrong with the way in which the report has been presented, the first being the manner in which the so-called profit for each division has been determined. Since it has been presented on a typical absorption basis of accounting, a method which calls for the complete absorption or allocation of common overhead expenses, additional information would be needed to unravel these costs and to put the operating side of the report into proper perspective. An examination of the operating detail, for example, might disclose the following background information:

Cost of Sales   The manufacturing cost of goods sold has been determined as follows:

1. Direct variable manufacturing cost per unit:

Division A	$3.60
Division B	6.00
Division C	2.00

2. Period manufacturing expenses (fixed overhead) of $300,000 for the year are common to all products produced and were allocated to divisions on the basis of the number of units produced and sold.

Selling Expense   The total selling expense of $150,000 for the year has been distributed to each of the three divisions on the basis of the net dollar volume of sales, and includes the following general categories of expense:

General Selling Expense	$60,000
Advertising, Division A	20,000
Promotion, Division B	30,000
Distribution, Division C	40,000

Administrative Expense The total of $100,000 in administrative expense has been distributed to each of the three divisions as a percent of the cost of sales.

When the operating statement is then resubmitted with the fixed and variable costs and expenses properly analyzed and identified, a presentation on the basis of direct costing will begin to lead to some quite opposite interpretations of the "profit" results for the year, as Table 2 shows.

Table 2

	Division A	Division B	Division C	Total
Units Sold	50,000	30,000	20,000	100,000
Price, $	8.00	15.00	7.50	10.00
Net Sales, $	400,000	450,000	150,000	1,000,000
Direct Cost of Sales, $	180,000	180,000	40,000	400,000
Gross Margin, $	220,000	270,000	110,000	600,000
P/V Ratio, %	55.0	60.0	73.0	60.0
Assignable Period Expense				
Selling Expense, $	20,000	30,000	40,000	90,000
Profit Contribution, $	200,000	240,000	70,000	510,000
Percent to Sales	50.0	53.0	47.0	51.0
Nonassignable Period Expense				
Manufacturing				$300,000
Selling				60,000
Administrative				100,000
Total				$460,000
Pretax Profit				50,000
Income Taxes				25,000
Net Earnings				$ 25,000

The measurements provided by this new statement now suggest the following:

1. The gross margin on sales for each division now presents a constant relationship of profit to volume, a measurement expressed as the P/V ratio, or percent to sales. Since it has been freed of the effect of fixed cost absorption, it can now be considered linear with volume and can serve as a reliable measurement of the profit leverage inherent in higher volume. On this basis, Division C now presents the greatest profit potential for growth.

2. The new statement also measures in each divisional report only those elements of fixed overhead, now identified as Assignable Period Expense, which exist solely in support of the operations of each division and are not common to the business as a whole. The resulting measurement of Profit Contribution then identifies the relative contribution of each division at this level of volume toward the recovery of corporate overhead and total operating profit. On this basis, Division B now appears to be the most profitable of the three, at a 53% rate of profit contribution—a level, however, which is now only slightly ahead of Division A, the operation previously reported at a loss and earmarked for early extinction.

Thus freed of the effects of arbitrary cost allocations, the accounting concept of profit is discarded in favor of the measurement of profit contribution, a valid operating evaluation of divisional results which puts the measurement on a "stand alone" basis not dependent upon the shared costs and shared performance of other operations. And for those who might protest that the "profit contribution" does not include any portion of the necessary support of the common overheads for the manufacturing, selling, or administrative functions of the business, it would be well to consider the purpose for which the measurement is being made. If the profit measurement is to serve as no more than a historical record of completed transactions, then perhaps the assessment of shared costs will reflect an estimated apportionment of corporate expense that might be judged as having "belonged" to each divisional operation.

If, on the other hand, the measurement is to serve as a guide to better decision making and increased profitability for the future, it would seem preferable to measure the results from operations in such a way that action might be taken in the area that offered the greatest potential for profit improvement. To accomplish this, the level of relative contribution would obviously be more indicative of future potential than would an allocated recording of interdependent results. Use of the profit contribution concept of operating results as a relative measure of profitability should also give recognition to the fact that by leaving out the allocation of common overheads, the "missing" cost is in fact *effectively included in the resulting higher rate* of profit contribution required.

As a measurement of the true profitability of divisional operations, however, the statement is not complete until the profit contribution for each of the several divisions has also been measured against the proportionate amount of investment that it took to produce the earnings. This, in turn, is measured in terms of the average investment required in Assets Managed, a measurement of those assets directly under the control of divisional management where both the authority and the responsibility for investment can be measured directly. And, as in the case of the operating figures, it should be a "stand alone" type of measurement, one not contaminated by arbitrary allocations of common resources over which division management has no authority and no control. Using this approach, it might then be found that the assets managed for each of the three operating divisions showed the following average levels of investment for the year:

	Division A	Division B	Division C
Inventories	$60,000	$100,000	$40,000
Receivables	35,000	75,000	15,000
Assets Managed	$95,000	$175,000	$55,000

When these values are then added to the report, combining the operating measurement of Profit Contribution with the measurement of Assets Managed, the resulting evaluation of Return on Assets Managed would not only present a final and valid measurement of true profitability for each division, but also would then lead to some completely viable conclusions and decisions regarding the probable future of each divisional operation, as shown in Table 3.

The operations of Division A are now viewed not as a loss operation but as the most profitable of the three divisions of the company. For while the gross margin rate, or P/V ratio, properly reflects the relationship of volume to profit, and while the level of profit contribution further measures the dollar amount contributed by each operation at that particular level of volume, the final measurement of true profitability is not determined until the operating results are also linked with the use of capital employed, which in this case is the portion of the capital under divisional control in the form of assets managed.

In summary, the Return on Assets measurement of profit finds a useful place in management reporting when it is applied not to total assets and total accounted earnings for the business as a whole but to the measurement of profit center operations within the company. To be used properly at this level, the concept of profit contribu-

Table 3

	Division A	Division B	Division C	Total
Units Sold	50,000	30,000	20,000	100,000
Unit Price, $	8.00	15.00	7.50	10.00
Net Sales, $	400,000	450,000	150,000	1,000,000
Direct Cost of Sales, $	180,000	180,000	40,000	400,000
Gross Margin, $	220,000	270,000	110,000	600,000
P/V Ratio, %	55.0	60.0	73.0	60.0
Assignable Period Expense				
Selling Expense, $	20,000	30,000	40,000	90,000
Profit Contribution, $	200,000	240,000	70,000	510,000
Percent to Sales	50.0	53.0	47.0	51.0
Assets Managed				
Inventories	$ 60,000	$100,000	$40,000	$200,000
Receivables	35,000	75,000	15,000	125,000
Total	$ 95,000	$175,000	$55,000	$325,000
Return on Assets				
Managed, %	210.0	137.0	127.0	157.0
Nonassignable Period Expense				
Manufacturing				$300,000
Selling				60,000
Administrative				100,000
Total				$460,000
Pretax Profit				50,000
Income Taxes				25,000
Net Earnings				$ 25,000

tion must be substituted for the accounting measurement
of profit, and the appraisal of total asset investment must
be discarded in favor of the more meaningful measurement of specific assets managed by each operating activity. When used in this fashion, the concept of linking
profit to asset investment becomes both a subordinate

[45]

and a fully integrated part of the measurement of return on invested capital for the company as a whole. Individual rates of return for each profit center can thus be compared in terms of relative profitability against the composite rate of return on assets managed in total. The composite rate, in turn, then describes the attainment required at this level of operations to satisfy the final demand for return on capital when all other financial elements of cost and investment have been accounted for. And since the Return on Assets Managed measurement frequently covers the more immediately controllable elements of volume, price, cost, and investment, it also frequently becomes the focal point for leverage in the management of return on invested capital itself.

three

Return on equity

A THIRD MEASUREMENT OF PROFIT, and one which is far more popular in common usage than either return on assets or return on invested capital, is the profit measurement known as the Return on Equity. It is found fairly frequently in the published financial reports of the larger publicly held companies, and where used seems to be offered as a sort of supporting measurement for the earnings per share report, or perhaps as evidence of a further proof of profitability in relating the reported earnings to an investment base.

The return on equity is calculated by taking the accounted or net book earnings for the period as a percentage rate of return on *only the equity portion* of the total invested capital of the business. The resulting measurement is often described as an evaluation of how well management has done in managing the stockholders' investment in the company, and is regarded by some as the ultimate test of corporate profitability. And since the accounted net earnings, after the deduction of any interest expense on debt capital, do in fact represent the full net return to the equity investor, the logic of the Return on Equity measurement appears difficult to refute. It is, as has been noted, a "return on investment" type of profit measurement. It also has the virtue of not overstating the investment base, or—within the limits of what it purports to do—of understating the earnings for the period. Since the investment base is quite specifically described as the total of the equity capital to be found on the balance sheet, there is no confusion in measurement as between capital and assets, no vehicle by which the assets provided by the noninterest-bearing operating debt can be thrown into the investment total. It is also intended to represent a measurement of the net earnings accruing to the equity shareholder, and as such the use of accounted net earnings after deduction of interest charges is at least completely relevant to the measurement being developed. These virtues aside, however, the return on equity measurement can, and frequently does, provide one of the most misleading measurements of profit currently used in business.

As noted, the logic of the measurement appears difficult to refute—difficult until the question is raised of *just how much the return on equity ought to be*, either for a given company at any one point in time or as a relative measure over a period of time for any business under changing ratios of debt to equity in the capital structure.

For, unlike the profit measurement of return on invested capital, the rate of return on equity does not normally represent an overall evaluation of the economic rate of return, *nor does it contain to any useful degree a qualitative measurement of what the rate of return ought to be as compensation for risk.* Since it omits the evaluation or use of debt capital in the investment base, the return on equity measurement rests on the assumptions that the cost of debt capital is fully satisfied by the amount of interest paid, and that anything earned by the use of debt over and above the interest cost represents an economic gain for the equity investor. Inherent in this reasoning, therefore, is also the assumption that the total capital employed in the business has in fact *two separate costs*—the cost of debt and the cost in terms of an earnings requirement for the equity—costs which then depend on the *source* of the funds employed rather than on the use to which they are put.

If this reasoning is to be followed, then it must also be apparent that the entire earnings requirement of the business as compensation for risk is being compressed and measured solely against the equity investment itself, a base that will obviously diminish in relative size as the debt ratio is increased. In spite of this, it may be argued that as long as increasing amounts of debt capital can be presumed to provide income somewhere in excess of the interest cost, that the so-called leveraging of results will also quite obviously leverage the rate of return on equity, oftentimes quite dramatically, and that the added "profit" to the shareholder is simply evidence of astute management which has found a cheap source of capital in the use of borrowed funds. If at the same time it is also pointed out that the increasing rate of return thus reported on the equity seems to be providing a favorable reaction in the short-term behavior of the market price for shares, the question is quite naturally raised as to where the weakness or fallacy in such a measurement might be. What can be said to be wrong with the idea of using borrowed money if it can produce a profit?

The answer, of course, is that there is absolutely nothing wrong with the concept of using debt capital to produce a profit, provided it does indeed produce a true economic profit for the business and not just the appearance of profit as judged by a hybrid method of reporting. The fallacy of the use of the Return on Equity measurement of profit lies in its failure to identify the *adequacy* of the earnings and the fact that the risk factor is nowhere inherent in the rate of return reported. By running contrary to the principle that the total cost of total capital used in business is ultimately determined by the risk at which it is employed, and not by where the funds come from, the measurement ignores the fact that the leveraged rate of return has also leveraged the risk to the equity shareholder in direct proportion to the apparent increase in earnings. The reported gains are not, unfortunately, a one-way street, but respond very closely to the law of physics that states that for every action there is an equal and opposite reaction.

Debt capital is not an isolated entity or separable piece of the capital structure that can stand alone or whose economic cost can be measured simply in terms of the rate of interest or in the total amount of interest payments to be made. It is, first of all, a segment of the total capital that depends entirely on the foundation of the equity investment for its very existence. Without a solid base of equity capital a company would have no borrowing power, no debt capacity by which interest-bearing funds could be employed. The equity base thus creates the availability of debt, a sequence which makes the two completely interwoven into a common pattern and common purpose of supplying the total funds used in business. As a common resource, capital is thus made up of a combination of debt and equity, a combination which becomes mutually interdependent, with the amount of equity determining the availability of debt, and the level of debt in turn determining both the ultimate risk and changing cost of the equity. Leveraging, in short, leverages both the rate of return and the risk to the equity at an equal and constant rate.

This interdependence perhaps becomes most evident when the relationship of debt to equity is examined in a step-by-step process, a process which will serve to identify the impact of debt on the attendant risk to the equity shareholder. As a starting point, Figure 1 illustrates the position of a company whose capital is made up of 100% equity investment, and one which is further assumed to have an average risk factor requiring a net 10.0% after-tax rate of return on total capital, a figure which can be equated to an approximate 20.0% pretax rate of return for all practical purposes.

Under these conditions, the cost of total capital and the cost or rate of return required on the equity capital

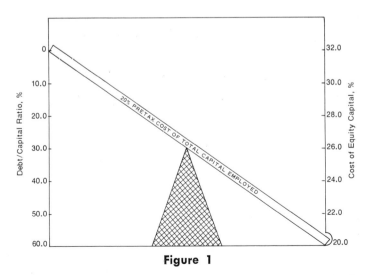

Figure 1

coincide at the same 20% rate, since equity and total capital are one and the same. It is also at this point and at this point alone that the Return on Equity measurement of profit fully measures the true economic rate of return for the business, since all capital employed is represented by the equity and since—with zero debt—the accounted net earnings also represent the total stream of earnings on the investment. Under these rather limited conditions, in other words, the profit measurements of return on equity and return on invested capital become synonymous.

When the capital structure is changed, however, the identity is lost and the return on equity *requirement* will be seen to be a function of the amount and type of debt used. If the picture is changed to assume a capital structure of 20.0% debt and 80.0% equity, a more normal configuration for the average business, the movement of the bar over the fulcrum will then suggest a corresponding increase in the cost or rate of return required on the equity. In doing so, it is assumed that the increasing use of debt will not change the overall risk of the business and that the risk cost of total capital will remain a constant at the pretax rate of 20.0% indicated for the average business, an assumption not usually warranted as the level of debt capital approaches the maximum borrowing capacity, as Figure 2 demonstrates.

Following the proposition that leveraging will leverage both the rate of return and the risk to the equity at an equal and constant rate, Figure 2 indicates that the use of 20.0% debt in the capital structure could leverage the return on equity to a typical 24.0% pretax rate of return, and that the risk to the equity investor—and hence the cost of equity capital in terms of earnings requirements—has likewise increased to the 24.0% level. While the factors contributing to this increased risk on the part of the equity may not be immediately evident, they are never-

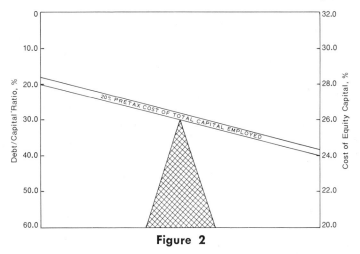

Figure 2

theless present and beginning to exert an upward force
on the earnings demand. If this first layer of debt,
amounting to 20.0% of the total capital employed, can
be assumed to be in the form of senior obligations of the
company, it might have been incurred as a mortgage note
for which the land and buildings of the corporation have
been pledged as collateral.

While the risk to the lender is thus secured in a measurable value of assets, the risk to the equity investor has
now taken at least a moderate increase on two counts:
First, his claim to such assets is now subordinated to that
of the bank in the event of liquidation, so that the present
value of his ownership investment has been lessened to a
degree. Perhaps more important, he is now sharing the
operating earnings of the business with the moneylend-
ers, with a certain portion of current income now dedicated to cover interest payments. He also recognizes that
such interest payments will henceforth come off the top,
that is, must be met first, before he participates in any
earnings at all. Seeing this as a reverse sort of leverage
which will clearly work against him if the business should

turn down, he notes that his risk has again been raised, if only moderately. The change or increase to the risk and the cost of equity has, however, been set in motion and will continue to rise as the level of debt is increased.

Succeeding layers of debt will add to the level of assets pledged as well as to the increasing percentage of total earnings to be set aside to meet the heavier load of interest costs. The added risk to the equity investment, however, will not be confined to the inexorable impact of these two factors alone, but will take on new and greater dimensions as the debt continues to mount. Unsecured debt, borrowings which can no longer be covered with tangible assets as collateral, will next carry with it a wide-ranging list of *debt restrictions*, limitations imposed on operating management by the lender who now has a major stake in the results of the business and who has therefore moved into a position of effective control over the disbursement of funds.

Typical among such debt restrictions will be found a limitation on the payment of dividends, the maintenance of certain operating ratios with respect to working capital, limitations restricting the use of funds for the acquisition of new capital equipment or for increases in the levels of compensation together with a prohibition on the possibilities of merger or acquisition. Indeed, the third illustration—suggesting a probable 60.0% debt-to-capital limit on borrowing capacity for the average industrial company—is, if anything, conservative in indicating an increase to no more than 32.0% in the cost of equity. At this point the banks have first call on virtually all assets of the business, have severely limited the decision-making authority of operating management, and are literally in control of the business. The equity investor is now clearly last in line, both in the event of liquidation and with respect to participation in current earnings, as Figure 3 shows.

[54]

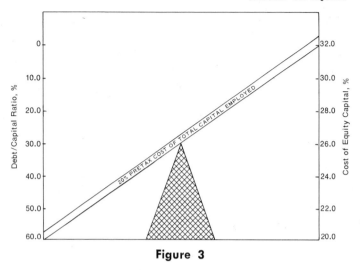

Figure 3

Why Return on Equity Is Used

The foregoing analysis might easily lead to the con-
clusion that the inherent weaknesses in the Return on
Equity measurement would be so readily apparent that
its use should be avoided or, at the very least, confined to
the role of a subordinate measurement perhaps linked to
the evaluation of the economic rate of return on capital.
But it is, as has been noted, one of the more popular forms
of profit measurement in current use in business. Why,
then, does business apparently cling to a measurement
that presents less than a total picture of profitability?
Why does management choose an indicator of profit that
is frequently more of a measurement of the extent of
corporate obligations than it is of managerial performance?

The answer must be presumed to lie in two basic directions: A lack of understanding of what the measurement means, what it omits, and what it implies can be
assumed to be one of the more obvious reasons for its use.

Since it gives the appearance of a fundamental index of profit measurement, a net rate of return on the ownership capital, it is quite possibly not challenged as to its adequacy by those who have adopted it. But behind this first group there must surely be a second, a group of managers who are well aware of the many implications of the measurement but who see a unique opportunity to be able to report continued progress in terms of "profitability," even when the overall results may be slowly deteriorating. The case of The Average Manufacturing Company (Chapter 1) may again serve to illustrate the point, where a reference to the figures already used will show the following:

	19X2	19X1	19X0
Equity Capital, $	12,500	11,500	10,500
Average Equity, $	12,000	11,000	
Accounted Earnings, $	1,410	1,240	
Return on Equity, %	11.8	11.3	

In this instance, a modest increase has been reported in the rate of return on equity, even though, as it will be recalled, the true profitability of the business had remained completely unchanged at a constant rate of a 10.0% return on invested capital. Realizing that it could thus report an apparent increase in earnings where no gain actually existed, management might then be inclined to examine the mathematics of this phenomenon a bit more closely and come up with the following analysis:

1. During the most recent year the company had employed average capital of $15,000, of which the interest-bearing debt had averaged $3,000, or only 20.0% of the total. Debt in the prior year, on the other hand, had averaged only $2,000, or a little over 15.0% of the capital employed.

[56]

2. Since the return on invested capital had remained constant at a net 10.0% rate of return, the greater use of debt was apparently responsible for the reported gain which showed up in the return on equity measurement.

3. The current debt load of only 20.0% of capital is immediately looked upon as being too conservative, and management speculates on what the "profit" results might have been if more debt had been used in place of equity capital during the past year. The *pro forma* statement in Table 4 is quickly prepared.

The message is abundantly clear. With no change whatsoever in the pretax operating profit from the business, and by simply doubling the debt and the interest expense, the reported "profit" could have been leveraged from an 11.8 to a 14.7% return on equity for the year. Feeling that the shareholders would certainly not have rejected the higher rate of return, management decisions begin to move in the direction of rapidly increasing the debt as a sure road to better profits. And if this is all that has been accomplished, the leveraging of the apparent

Table 4

	As Reported	Could Have Been
Average Debt	$ 3,000	$ 6,000
Average Equity	12,000	9,000
Average Capital	$15,000	$15,000
Operating Profit	$ 3,000	$ 3,000
Interest Expense	180	360
Pretax Profit	2,820	2,640
Income Taxes	1,410	1,320
Net Earnings	$ 1,410	$ 1,320
Return on Equity, %	11.8	14.7
Return on Capital, %	10.0	10.0

results without increasing the true net earnings of the business has obviously done nothing for the shareholder except to offer a misleading picture of results.

In the final analysis, the only true leveraging of profit occurs when *both* the return on equity and the return on invested capital gain from the profitable employment of debt capital. Such leveraging, the leveraging of profitable growth, makes economic sense when it takes advantage of opportunities which would be lost if dependent upon the gradual accumulation of equity capital through re-tained earnings. It makes economic sense to use borrowed capital when it can be put to work, not simply at a rate that provides something more than the interest cost but at a rate that satisfies the risk cost of total capital employed in the business. Such a measurement must recognize the profit requirement inherent in the rate of return on invested capital, the foundation from which the adequacy of the return on equity can be judged.

four

Return on sales

A FOURTH MEASUREMENT OF PROFIT, the rate of return on the dollar volume of sales, is a measurement which elects to confine the evaluation of profit solely to its relationship to volume, a measurement which thus completely ignores the entire question of how much investment it may have taken to produce either one. It is, however, widely used and even more widely misused, creating a false target for business and at the same time a complete misconception of the size and meaning of profit on the part of the general public.

The danger is great in both directions, for the management of the business and for the rather serious implications which the return on sales measurement has apparently created in the mind of the public. Where used in the larger companies with public ownership, the Percent Profit to Sales measurement is first used internally and then given emphasis in published annual reports—and then given further prominence in earnings statements summarized by the financial press. It is highlighted in such a way that the public, a large segment of which already believes that profits are either unnecessary or socially undesirable, is conditioned to accept the measurement as the final gauge of corporate profitability. With profits thus reported as being completely unrelated to the investment in capital required to produce them, the distinct impression is given, first of all, that the rates of return on sales are entirely relative in comparing one company with another. This erroneous impression was perhaps emphasized most explicitly in the following article, which appeared in a financial column of the *San Francisco Chronicle* on March 3, 1973, an "analysis" all too typical of many appearing in the press throughout the country.

> The earnings a company makes on its sales is called "profit margin" and it varies widely by industry. GM, for example, is earning 7.1 per cent on its prodigious sales volume—and that's well above the overall average.

> Contrast that performance with the showing of Safeway Stores . . . (who) rang up sales of $6 billion in 1972. Its after tax profit: $91 million. This means that Safeway gets to keep a cent and a half of every dollar that passes through its checkout cash registers.

> Petroleum companies won't settle for that kind of return. Standard Oil of California . . . collected a little bit more

money than Safeway in 1972—$6.7 billion—but its profits, $547 million, were six times as great.

General Electric . . . is adept at squeezing out profits. The country's largest electrical manufacturer earned $471 million in 1972 on sales of $10.2 billion.

For prowess in generating profits out of sales dollars, one company stands out as a super star, in a class by itself. That would be International Business Machines Corp., the undisputed leader of the computer industry.

IBM's sales last year were $9.5 billion, placing it just below General Electric . . . however, on that volume IBM earned $1.2 billion after taxes, nearly three times what GE did.

All in all, a confusing report that switches from percentages to dollars of earnings, from which the reader must make his own rate of return calculations if he is expected to get some picture of comparative performance —but a report which also clearly suggests a finite measurement of profitability in the figures presented. In summary, the article has drawn a picture of relative "profit" performance which might be tabulated as follows:

Company	Return on Sales, %
IBM	12.6
Standard Oil of California	8.2
General Motors	7.1
General Electric	4.6
Safeway Stores	1.5

In making such a comparison, the article has suggested that IBM is by far the most profitable of the five companies listed, a superstar, and also that its profits were three times as great as those of General Electric. Since the 7.1% earned by General Motors is further referred to as "well above the overall average," it also implies that the earnings of both IBM and Standard Oil of California must therefore be unreasonably high. By contrast, Safeway Stores, which "gets to keep a cent and a half of every dollar," is pictured as a company with exceptionally poor profit performance, one barely breaking even in doing some $6 billion in sales.

What is omitted, of course, and what was either not understood or possibly overlooked by the author of the article, is that the report of earnings as a percent of sales is but *one-half of the measurement of profitability*—a half that has virtually no meaning until it is linked with the amount of investment behind the earnings, the amount of capital employed to produce them. To put this in perspective, it is first of all necessary to see how much capital was required to support the volume of sales reported and to identify the *turnover rate*, or relationship of volume to investment:

Company	Sales (in billions)	Invested Capital (in billions)	Turnover
IBM	$9.5	$7.0	1.4
Standard Oil of California	6.7	5.9	1.1
General Motors	30.4	12.2	2.5
General Electric	10.2	3.2	3.2
Safeway Stores	6.0	0.6	9.6

This analysis discloses that the *need for capital* is apparently quite different among these five companies. Standard Oil of California, a highly capital intensive type of business, can support only $1.10 in sales for every $1.00 of capital employed in the company, while Safeway Stores, an entirely different industry, does a volume of $9.60 in sales for every $1.00 invested in the business. Such differences in the need for capital would then seem to indicate a possible difference in the need for the rate of earnings on the sales dollar itself, with the lower rates of capital turnover setting up a demand for a higher rate of return on sales, and vice versa. When these two controlling factors are then brought together, the true profitability of the five companies quoted in the article takes on a quite different perspective, one which leads to some quite opposite conclusions:

Company	Return on Sales, %	Turnover	Return on Capital, %
General Motors	7.1	2.5	17.8
IBM	12.6	1.4	17.2
General Electric	4.6	3.2	14.8
Safeway Stores	1.5	9.6	14.5
Standard Oil of California	8.2	1.1	9.3

One final comparison will perhaps suffice to discredit the claims of "profit" based on the comparison of return on sales alone. Standard Oil of California, whose profits were said to be six times as great as those of Safeway Stores, actually shows a level of profitability only two-thirds as good when fully measured on the basis of return on invested capital. And petroleum companies, very plainly, can *not* afford to settle for a 1.5% return on sales, not with nearly ten times the invested capital employed by the supermarkets.

The need for a heavier investment in capital is plainly inherent in some types of industry—those typically referred to as "capital intensive" types of business—and with it an also inherent need for a rate of return on sales that will in turn justify this greater use of investment. Other industries have far less need for capital in relation to the total volume of sales, and the resulting higher turnover of investment also requires far less profit on each dollar of volume to satisfy the same basic profitability requirement. These two supporting measurements, the turnover of capital coupled with the rate of return on sales, form a natural set of parameters which must be recognized for a particular industry, since the operating objectives for one will be vastly different from another. They do, however, have a common meeting ground in the overall need for an adequate return on invested capital, a common minimum objective that is perhaps best illustrated by Figure 4.

A second implication suggested by this type of reporting is that the profits of many companies are simply too high, a suggestion quite strongly planted in the final paragraph of the article when the author suddenly switches from after-tax earnings to pretax profits and states that, "IBM's profits before taxes were $2.4 billion, which means it's operating on a gross profit margin of better than 25 per cent. It makes a buck on every four dollars of sales. With its hold on the computer market, IBM is truly a money-making machine."

This type of financial reporting would appear to do little to instill confidence and understanding in the basic elements of the profit system, and could easily give rise

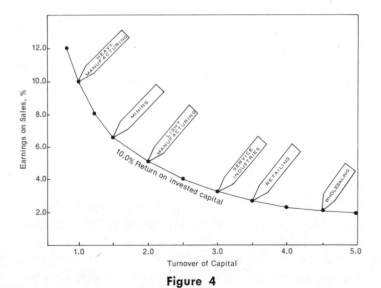

Figure 4

to the growing popular belief that such profits should, in fact, be limited by government regulation. It is at least conceivable that articles of this type have given some support to the public misconception of profits found in a survey conducted during 1971 by the Opinion Research Corporation of Princeton, New Jersey, which asked the question: "Just as a rough guess, what per cent profit on each dollar of sales do you think the average manufacturer makes after taxes?" This question was asked of the public at large, including some investors, whose median estimate was given in an answer of *28.0% of the sales dollar, after taxes.* Not too surprisingly, fully one-third of those polled also felt that the federal government should take action to limit such profits.

Two basic facts have thus escaped the general public: the first, that after-tax profits on sales average something less than 5.0%, not 28.0%, and second, that whatever the rate of return on sales might be, it cannot be judged as either high or low if taken by itself, and that its adequacy or degree of profitability depends entirely on the level of capital employed in the business. These rather elementary steps in financial education, however, cannot be expected to start with keener insight on the part of the general public or with further analysis on the part of the occasional investor. The process must start at the source, with the corporate manager, who has the dual responsibility of using the proper measurement of profit for his own guidance and of presenting a complete profit story to the outside world. By not doing so, business is not only creating its own false objectives and targets for accomplishment but, perhaps even more importantly, is also creating its own growing and rather formidable opposition to the entire profit system.

The average corporate manager will not, however, be alerted to take action in what he may regard as the field of financial public relations until he is first convinced of the seriousness of the situation in his own company. If he has been using a Return on Sales measurement as the primary financial evaluation of results, it is also fair to assume that he has been making serious attempts to improve it—attempts that could succeed in reaching such limited objectives while gradually eroding the earning power of the company. He could, by the very process of forcing up the return on sales, be reporting apparent increases in corporate earnings that represented no more than a gradual liquidation of corporate capital.

The figures already used several times for The Average Manufacturing Company (Chapter 1) will again serve to illustrate the point. In its most recent year the company had reported net earnings of $1,410 on $30,000 of sales, a rate of return of 4.7%. The following plans have been discussed to increase this rate substantially in the coming year, in the belief that this is the direction a proper · conduct of the business should dictate:

1. The average bank debt of only $3,000 amounts to no more than 20.0% of the total capital of $15,000 employed in the business. This is considered far too modest, and the proposal has been made to triple it to $9,000 immediately.

2. The added cash of $6,000 to be received from new borrowings plus the cash generated by depreciation charges and expected earnings on higher volume will provide room for carrying a greater investment in both inventory and accounts receivable.

3. It is estimated that sales will jump 10.0% in volume if inventories are doubled to provide immediate delivery from stock and if sales terms are extended to net 60 days, a move which would also approximately double the investment in accounts receivable.

4. Since the direct variable costs associated with volume are found to be only 50.0% of sales, the

increased profit to be expected from a 10.0% increase in sales is projected as given in Table 5.

Management would now appear to have an excellent plan for a rapid and substantial gain in profits—jumping to a 6.0% rate of return on sales—with the added interest expense on the increased debt load more than covered by the expected gain in operating margin. At the end of the year the objective has been reached, the higher return on sales achieved, and management is congratulating itself on the improved performance it is about to report to the shareholders when it is suddenly confronted with a report which has been prepared by its new controller, as in Table 6.

This new report points out, rather disturbingly, that the increased rate of return on sales to 6.0% for the year just ended required an additional investment of $11,000 in working capital, which produced a net return of only 6.8% after taxes. It also states that since the cost of capital for the company is considered to be a minimum of 10.0%, that the 6.8% return on the new investment had actually resulted in a loss of capital of $350, or nearly

Table 5

	Prior Year	Projected
Sales	$30,000	$33,000
Gross Margin	15,000	16,500
Period Expense	12,000	12,000
Operating Profit	3,000	4,500
Interest Expense	180	540
Pretax Profit	2,820	3,960
Net Earnings	$ 1,410	$ 1,980
Percent of Sales	4.7	6.0

Table 6

	Last Year	This Year	Increase
Sales	$30,000	$33,000	$ 3,000
Accounted Net Earnings	1,410	1,980	570
Net Interest Cost	90	270	180
Total Earnings	$ 1,500	$ 2,250	$ 750
Average Capital Employed			
Cash	$ 750	$ 750	—
Accounts Receivable	3,750	7,550	$ 3,800
Inventory	7,200	14,400	7,200
Fixed Assets	6,000	6,000	—
Prepaid Expenses	2,300	2,300	—
Total Assets	$20,000	$31,000	$11,000
Operating Debt	(5,000)	(5,000)	—
Invested Capital	$15,000	$26,000	$11,000
Return on Invested Capital, %	10.0	8.7	6.8

one-half of the reported "gain" in earnings, a gain that
had been attained for the company by the liquidation of
its own capital. This latter point is then illustrated by
showing the profit requirement *as a cost of doing
business*, a cost which has not been recovered by the
company:

	Last Year	This Year
Average Capital Employed	$15,000	$26,000
Cost of Capital @ 10.0%	1,500	2,600
Total Earnings	1,500	2,250
Loss of Capital	—	$(350)

The concept of measuring profit as a percentage rate
of return on sales is seldom confined to the corporate
or total company level—where the effects might thus be
quickly seen and perhaps readily corrected through a

series of new top management decisions—but generally spreads as a philosophy to the middle and lower levels of management where the effects are not always so readily discernible. If the corporate reporting has, in fact, been geared to the return on sales measurement of profit, it is quite likely that operating budgets and goals for the various divisions, branches, or product-line segments of the business have also been set in the same framework. Operating management has thus, to all intents and purposes, been conditioned to respond in a myriad of decisions that will be made in an attempt to maximize the profit measurement used by the company. The unfortunate part of this chain reaction is that the decisions taken in this direction will generally be submerged from view in the process of delegation of authority, a delegation made necessary in the larger companies by the very size and complexity of the business. They will be submerged as the basis for decision making at all levels of management so that finally only the overall results will be measurable, and not the reasons or judgments which served to bring them about. The effect will multiply rapidly throughout a large organization, pyramiding the misuse of the profit measurement and leading to results which can eventually weaken the entire earning power of the business.

Such decisions at the profit center level may take several forms. If, for example, this philosophy of management had prevailed in the case of the company with the three operating divisions, discussed when dealing with the Return on Assets measurement (Chapter 2), the operations of Division A might well have been phased out, since it was showing a negative rate of return on sales. Or, alternately, more assets might have been committed in support of Division C in an attempt to raise the return on sales, even though the division already had the heaviest tie-up of investment and the lowest rate of

[69]

Table 7

Per Unit	Division A	Division B	Division C	Total
Total Manufacturing Cost	$6.60	$ 9.00	$5.00	$ 7.00
Selling and Administrative	2.14	3.55	1.83	2.50
Total Cost per Unit	$8.74	$12.55	$6.83	$ 9.50
Cost Divided by 90.0%				
= Price	9.70	13.95	7.60	10.55
Price Charged	$8.00	$15.00	$7.50	$10.00

return on assets managed. But perhaps more significantly, the return on sales goal may be used as the target rate in pricing decisions, one of the most sensitive areas in any business and one which will ultimately affect not only profits, but volume, cost, and investment as well.

If the pricing in this company were based, as it so often is in many actual situations, on an arbitrary target of a pretax rate of a 10.0% return on sales, a pricing review based on the original operating statement might have been made as in Table 7.

Following this approach, the average pricing in Division A would be increased by over 20.0%, from $8.00 to $9.70; Division B products reduced from $15.00 to $13.95; and the Division C average left virtually unchanged in going from $7.50 to $7.60 a unit. Whether or not these new prices were then more competitive, however, the method used would not have succeeded in meeting the profit requirements of the company. If, on the other hand, pricing had been based on a return on investment approach to profit objectives rather than on the partial measurement afforded by the return on sales target, the pricing decisions might have taken quite a different form, with more positive results. Such an approach would then have included the following steps:

1. The profit target for the business has been set as a net 15.0% return on invested capital after taxes.
2. The level of average capital employed is estimated at $600,000.
3. A 15.0% return on $600,000 of invested capital would dictate a net earnings requirement of $90,000 after taxes, or a pretax profit level of $180,000.
4. With fixed overhead in the form of period expenses for the manufacturing, selling, and administrative functions totaling $460,000 a year, a profit contribution of $640,000 a year would be required to yield the pretax book profit of $180,000.
5. With a total of $325,000 in assets managed by divisional operations, an average rate of return of approximately 200% would be required at this level of measurement if pricing were to meet the profit objectives of the company.

With this as background for its pricing decisions, the average prices of the three divisions would then be computed as shown in Table 8.

Prices determined in this manner will now give management some useful tools for decision making:

Table 8

	Division A	Division B	Division C	Total
Assets Managed	$ 95,000	$175,000	$ 55,000	$ 325,000
200% Return Required	190,000	350,000	110,000	650,000
Add Period Expenses	20,000	30,000	40,000	90,000
Gross Margin Required	210,000	380,000	150,000	740,000
Add Direct Variable Cost	180,000	180,000	40,000	400,000
Sales Volume Required	$390,000	$560,000	$190,000	$1,140,000
Unit Sales	50,000	30,000	20,000	100,000
Unit Price Required	$7.80	$18.65	$ 9.50	$11.40

[71]

1. The prices computed are those actually required by current operating costs and levels of investment to enable the company to reach its full profit objective.

2. Assuming that a balanced product line is essential to the overall conduct of the business, the *average* price used in the volume and mix of products must yield a combined profit contribution of $650,000, or a 200% rate of return on the planned use of assets under divisional control. In other words, if a lower-than-indicated price were used in one area, higher prices must prevail in others in order to achieve the average required.

3. If the prices indicated by the calculation prove not to be competitive, management then has a clear measurement of the profit impact which would result from following such competitive prices, and with it also a clear measurement of the reduction needed in either cost or investment in order to make competitive pricing profitable.

In using an approach of this sort in the critical area of pricing, management would thus be giving recognition to a very basic concept of profit measurement, namely, that the rate of return on sales is not an end product in itself but simply a working tool to be used in reaching the objectives of fundamental profitability.

five

Dollars of profit

A FIFTH MEASUREMENT OF PROFIT, still apparently
in use in some companies, is the simple quantitative
use of the accounted net dollars of earnings as reported on the Profit and Loss Statement. Certainly
the Dollars of Profit evaluation has to be the oldest
form of profit measurement ever devised, no doubt
originating with earlier methods of cash accounting
as a means of business control. Before the concept
of double-entry bookkeeping was first introduced,
and with it a system of accruing both income and
related expenses for the period, many small busi-

nesses were run on a cash basis. If the contents of the cash drawer were greater at the end of the month than they were at the beginning, the increase was considered to be profit and expenditures for the ensuing period were planned accordingly.

The carry-over of this cash drawer measurement has apparently persisted in the attitude of looking at profit as what "is left," the bottom-line concept of black ink representing a profit and red ink a loss. And where it is used, it is inevitably tightly bound to both bookkeeping procedures and accounting systems. It is clearly a measurement of what the books show—no more or no less— and one which suggests also that management has next to no means of predicting the outcome of current operations but is entirely dependent upon the periodic "closing" of the books of account. At its very best, it is an after-the-fact measurement of sorts. At its worst, it does not even contain the basic elements required for the determination of profit. It has, in fact, all the sins and omissions already ascribed to many of the preceding measurements of profit, plus some peculiarities of its own. Unlike any of the Return on Investment measurement types of profit reporting, the use of profit dollars alone makes no attempt to link the so-called earnings with any form of investment required to produce them. And unlike the rate of return on sales, it also makes no attempt to relate the reported earnings to the volume of business transacted. It exists in a vacuum, having neither financial meaning nor any measurable connection with the rest of the business.

The implications for management planning and control are substantial. If it can be assumed that a company using the measurement of profit dollars were sufficiently sophisticated in other areas of financial management to have a program for long-range planning and budgeting, then it would follow that the financial objectives of the business were geared to the level of dollars alone, objectives which could easily result in the following pattern of performance over a period of time:

	1st Year	2d Year	3d Year	4th Year	5th Year
Net Profit, $	1,000	1,100	1,210	1,331	1,464
Rate of Increase, %	—	10.0	10.0	10.0	10.0
Invested Capital, $	10,000	12,500	15,500	20,000	25,000
Return on Capital, %	10.0	8.8	7.8	6.6	5.9

Assuming that no debt capital were used and that therefore no interest expense adjustment were necessary to relate the total earnings to the total capital employed, the company could readily have achieved an annual increase of 10.0% in reported dollars of profit while rapidly losing its own capital in a rate of return approaching no more than bank interest rates. This would also have to assume, of course, a steady inflow of new equity capital each year in addition to the retained earnings from operations, a proposition that might be supported during such a "growth" period but which would also quickly become untenable as investors began to evaluate the quality of the earnings record. While perhaps oversimplified for purposes of illustration, the preceding example is by no means an academic one, but unfortunately finds its counterpart in many actual situations where such a myopic view of the profit measurement prevails.

The obliviousness or complete disregard for the use and cost of capital employed would typically take many forms in the decision-making process aimed solely at increasing the reported dollars of profit. It might typically start with the cash management of the business, an area prone to mismanagement in many companies. Cash, in reality, is the least useful of all the assets on the Balance Sheet, having value only when it is put to work in the

[75]

operations of the business at a profitable rate of return. It is, of course, a highly necessary asset for the conduct of the business, and while it may be thought of as the lubricant that keeps the wheels of the business cycle in motion, it is not an asset to be hoarded by management or maintained in excess of its actual need. Good cash management, in fact, will operate with the lowest possible requirements consistent with meeting its obligations, turning cash some 40 times a year in relation to volume. Such action, however, implies a recognition on the part of management of the value of a complete integration of the financial elements of volume, profit, and investment, a recognition that will not be found in the company seeking only the target of dollars of earnings.

In quite the opposite direction, cash management in such a company will seek to use increasing amounts of cash to provide additional dollars in the profit column, regardless of the economics or rate of return consequences of the funds employed. It is not at all unusual, for example, to find an item on the balance sheets of many companies immediately following the cash account and identified as "marketable securities" or some such title, an item often representing a substantial investment of cash made by corporate management. If, in fact, it represents no more than a temporary investment of funds to be used in the near future for expansion and growth, it is an obviously sensible and intelligent way of producing additional income on monies which would otherwise be idled for the short term. If, however, the investment in such securities is not temporary, but more in the nature of a permanent use of surplus cash, as evidenced by the same item appearing regularly on the Balance Sheet time after time, then it must be assumed to have an entirely different meaning and different purpose.

Such "permanent" uses of the cash account, depending on the type of securities purchased, will yield no more than a 5.0% return at best, but quite obviously a 5.0% return on $1 million invested in this fashion will also add $50,000 to the pretax profits of the company, and will appear to be serving the cause well. No thought, of course, is given to the fact that the use of capital by management should produce a pretax return of at least 20.0% as compensation for the average risk—or that in committing a portion of its capital at a 5.0% return, the company is actually losing 15.0% of its investment in spite of the apparent gains recorded by accounted results. Corporate management, in short, has been given the capital to use in an industrial company and to provide a rate of return commensurate with an industrial risk. It has not been asked to divert part of the capital to run a mutual fund, although many managers would seem to be under such an impression.

The disregard for the use and cost of capital employed will then move to the area of customer Accounts Receivable, another fertile ground for generating additional dollars of profit. A proper management of this asset will also dictate a financial balance between investment and volume, between volume and profit, and between profit and investment, a complete integration of the elements involved in financial control. If two of these factors are to be ignored, however, and decisions made solely on the dollars of accounted profit reported, several steps can be taken to increase the latter—often substantially—at the expense of the former.

In most well-managed companies the terms of sale are an inherent part of the pricing structure, with the cost of funds to be tied up during the collection period and the amount of cash discount to be granted, if any, both included in the selling price of the product. With normal terms of 30 days net, one price would be used, and with terms of 60 or 90 days, higher prices would be charged to recover the cost of additional capital committed to the balance of trade receivables. If this also is to be ignored, as it would be in seeking to maximize only the dollars of profit, then no such constraints need exist, and sales terms could be generously extended to 180 days or more at no increase in price, with reasonable assurance that such a structure would attract more volume and add to the subsequent level of "profits." Along with this action, a general easing up of credit investigation and collection efforts would doubtless make the package more attractive and insure that no possible gains in accounted earnings were overlooked.

At this point the company would have badly mis-managed two of its major asset accounts in the quest for profit dollars. Perhaps a major share of the capital invested in the business would have been committed to securities— which the company may well be ill equipped to manage in any professional sense—as well as to an interest-free financing of its own customers' operations. The misuse of capital, however, will by no means stop at this point, not with the inventory account offering such a tempting target for further "improvement." Good inventory man-agement, again, will look to the balanced integration of financial results and will strive to maintain an optimum balance between the investment in inventory and what it can be expected to produce.

Typically, a larger investment in the average business than either the cash or the receivables, inventory is often given added attention by management, particularly with regard to its turnover rate related to volume and the earnings accruing from both. But again, if this basic consideration is to be cast aside, it will be found that more inventory will indeed provide more dollars of profit, often in several directions at once. For the business engaged in merchandising—in the purchase and sale of goods at either the retail or wholesale level—the attrac-tion of larger inventories might appear evident in two directions. Increased purchases in larger lots could first of all be counted on to reduce the unit price paid, an apparent profit gain at the input end of the business. At the same time, increased stocks on hand would generally assure better delivery prospects to the customer and thus contribute a second gain in recorded profits at the output end through higher volume. With such objectives, the cost of capital tied up is obviously of no concern to management, and the ultimate size of the inventory may be limited only by space considerations and the out-of-pocket carrying costs of the inventory itself.

For the manufacturing company, a third opportunity for profit gain in terms of dollars will present itself in addition to the first two. If inventories are to be increased, production must go up. And since higher production can generally be regarded as being more efficient, it can be assumed that costs will come down, a "profit improvement" that will clearly carry over to the net accounted results. The fact that the "profit from production" can also be readily manipulated through various types of cost accounting systems is by no means overlooked as a further avenue to short-term gains in the profit column.

It is perhaps only when the fourth major asset group is reached that the profit dollar approach to management seems to change direction. In making decisions for investment in new plant and equipment—land, buildings, and machinery—the same management that will completely disregard the use and cost of the working capital elements of the business will often impose an entirely different set of standards on the investment in fixed assets. Here, for some strange reason, the return on investment concept of profit is deemed essential, even going so far as to apply a discounted cash-flow measurement to recognize the time value of money. Commitments of new capital in this area are also quite stringently controlled, with management authority perhaps limited to a $10,000 or $15,000 level without higher approval, even in the larger companies. Since the same manager usually has complete freedom and authority to commit some hundreds of thousands of dollars to the working capital accounts of inventory and receivables—as long as it produces some added dollars of profit—it is a strange anomaly indeed. The particular restraint on capital equipment and its apparently singular requirement for a rate of return on investment would not appear to add a great deal of financial understanding for the individual manager concerned nor would it put the overall financial objectives and requirements of the business into any useful perspective.

This type of reporting also does little to dispel the popular public image of the huge profits apparently reported by business concerns. Even those companies that may actually be managed toward a more useful form of profit measurement will often fall back in published reports into accounts of the absolute dollars of earnings, referring to increases and percentage gains that give the impression of large profits even when, in many cases, the true profitability may be barely adequate or the profit dollars insufficient to cover the basic cost of risk capital. Nor is this type of confused reporting always avoided by the financial press. Even so prestigious a publication as *Forbes Magazine* apparently reverted to the profit dollars concept in an article entitled "The Great Imbalance" in the May 1, 1973, issue, which set forth the following proposition:

QUESTION: When is $2 billion worth four times $2 billion?

ANSWER: When you are dealing with a stock market that worships growth and sneers at solid earnings.

Here are some figures on 20 great American corporations, household names all. All are good companies, some superb.

	Sales	Net Income Before Extraordinary Items 1972	1968	Market Value 4/11/73
THE STANDARD GROUP				
Alcoa	$ 1,753	$ 103	$ 105	$ 1,156
Bank America	1,651	192	133	3,128
Chrysler	9,759	220	291	1,885
General Foods	2,424	113	103	1,324
Goodyear	4,071	193	148	1,981
ITT	8,600	477	204	4,099
Southern Pacific	1,449	108	88	963
Union Carbide	3,261	207	157	2,582
U.S. Steel	5,402	157	254	1,842
Westinghouse	5,087	199	135	3,348
TOTAL	$43,457	$1,969	$1,618	$22,308
THE GROWTH GROUP				
American Home Products	$ 1,587	$ 173	$ 112	$ 6,691
Avon	1,005	125	71	7,809
Coca-Cola	1,876	190	110	8,539
Eastman Kodak	3,478	546	375	22,940
Johnson & Johnson	1,318	121	50	6,979
Lilly	820	126	71	5,802
Merck	958	148	93	7,153
Minn. Mining & Mfg.	2,114	244	167	9,617
Polaroid	571	43	59	4,369
Xerox	2,419	250	129	12,059
TOTAL	$16,146	$1,966	$1,237	$91,958

All numbers in millions.

Group I has combined earnings of nearly $2 billion. Combined sales of $43 billion. Group II has combined earnings of nearly $2 billion. Combined sales of $16 billion.

Equal in earnings, the two groups are worlds apart in market value. Group I sells for a combined $22 billion, 11 times earnings. Group II sells for $92 billion, 46 times earnings.

[81]

How account for the $70 billion difference?

The $70 billion is the premium that the current invest-ment bias puts on so-called growth. Group I consists of profitable but slow-growing companies. Group II is all growth and glamour.

Is $1 worth of *growth* earnings worth close to $4 in *cyclical* earnings? The stock market says so. But the stock market isn't always right, not in the long run.

Our statisticians did a little more work. They went back five years. They found that five years ago the Standard Ten had earned a combined $1.6 billion. Their earnings grew 22% over the period. The Growth Ten earned about $1.2 billion. Their earnings grew about 59% over the same period.

The difference is there, but how big? The gap in the earnings growth between the two groups was only about $380 million. Assuming that the growth differentials hold, five years from now the growth group will be earning maybe $3.1 billion, the standard group maybe $2.6 billion. That $500 million differential is by no means in the bank, however; it could turn out to be less. Never-theless, current prices say that the prospective earnings differential is worth a premium of $70 billion to those who buy the stocks now.

Can a potential $500 million in earnings flow five years from now be worth $70 billion in cash today? If the answer is no, then one of three things must be true: Either the growth stocks are terribly overpriced, the standard stocks are terribly underpriced, or both.

In the *Forbes* article, the similarity of a $2 billion in reported dollars of earnings for each group is obviously the basis for comparison, a comparison which first sug-gests equality in earnings and then questions the vast dif-ference in market value as between $22 billion for the first group and $92 billion for the second. If the profitability of the two groups could actually be measured in dollars alone, the $70 billion difference would doubtless have to be "all growth and glamour." But something is quite obviously missing from the analysis, something which makes a fundamental difference in the concept and measurement of profit. The amount of invested capital required to produce the same $2 billion of earnings in each group is somewhat different—in fact, substantially different both in amount and in the consequent rate of return. A more useful comparison of the two groups would show that the "standard" group, as it is called, needed three times the capital employed by the "growth" group to produce the same level of dollars of income, as the following computation shows.

	Sales	Income	Invested Capital	Return on Capital
Standard Group	$43,457	$1,969	$29,700	6.6%
Growth Group	16,146	1,966	10,000	19.7%

The article states that the second group is selling at a combined market value of $92 billion, or a little over four times the $22 billion market price for shares of the first group. With equal dollars of earnings, the price differential is suggested as a possible overvaluation of the so-called growth stocks or undervaluation of the standard group. Whatever the total valuation ought to be at any point in time is, of course, the judgment of the investor, a judgment which perhaps views the results a bit differently. In this case the fact that the differential of four to one in market value is also closely paralleled by a three to one edge in the rate of return on invested capital is perhaps more than a passing coincidence. If anything, it could be said that any overvaluation present might be found in the "standard" group—a group of companies with a price earnings multiple of 11:1 earning only 6.6%

[83]

on invested capital, a rate of return hardly commensurate with the risk.

In summary, there are two fundamental aspects to any useful measurement of profit, the quantitative and the qualitative. Each of the several measurements in common use provides some sort of a quantitative evaluation of profit, either as a specific level or as a rate of return. The accounting process makes the dollars of profit the simplest evaluation of all, since by not being related to anything else it requires no further calculations or adjustments. The plain fact, however, that it fails to serve management in any way throughout the process of planning, operating, and controlling is thus finally demonstrated in the one area where it eventually counts the most, in the valuation of the business itself. Management may choose to disregard the use and cost of capital in its preoccupation with accounted results of profit dollars. The investor will not, and in the final analysis will look to the quality of earnings in making a true assessment of profit.

six

Earnings per share

A SIXTH MEASUREMENT OF PROFIT commonly used in business, the one which is by far the most popular with the larger companies whose shares are widely held by the public, is the measurement of Earnings per Share.

Unlike most of the several measurements of profit already described, the Earnings per Share measurement does not relate the earnings for the period to any form of investment or to any value for the dollar volume of sales transacted by the company. By comparison, it is actually a great deal closer to the

Dollars of Profit measurement than it is to any other. In its simplest form, it merely takes the net accounted or reported earnings for the period and divides them by the average number of shares of stock outstanding, thus measuring "profit" in terms of the number of pieces of paper which evidence the ownership of the equity and hence the ownership of the reported earnings.

In practice, of course, it becomes a bit more complex. Since the report of earnings per share is understood to refer to the earnings for a single share of common stock or common equity of the company, the first step in those companies which also carry preferred stock is to deduct the stipulated preferred earnings from the accounted total to determine the net earnings available for the common. In many companies, it also then takes on a second complexity, that of being reported in two different ways at the same time. For those companies which also have a layer of convertible debt capital as a part of the investment structure, the earnings per share on the common are reported first as the "primary" earnings, based on the average number of shares actually issued. A second report is then issued for the earnings per share on a "fully diluted" basis, a lower figure, to reflect the potential dilution arising from the conversion of debt to equity. Since the convertible debt of such a company may thus be exchanged for additional shares of common stock under certain specified conditions, the "fully diluted" report of earnings per share thus reports the earnings results on a consolidated basis of combining the number of actual shares and the number of potential shares into a common pool. In doing this, the process makes the interesting admission that the convertible debt and the common equity must be considered as a single entity or pool of invested capital for purposes of measurement—a concept which has already been suggested in the need for measuring *all*

[86]

capital as a common resource with both a common risk and a common cost.

In concept, the idea of reporting and measuring earnings on the basis of so many dollars and cents per share of common stock would appear to have both logic and the merit of simplicity in its favor. The argument for logic would be the very obvious one that the earnings so reported do in fact legally *belong* to the equity shareholder and to no one else. Interest on any debt capital which may have been used by the company has already been paid for and reflected in the lower net earnings reported, and the remainder is clearly the legal property of the common shareholder, whether he receives it in current dividends or whether it is plowed back into the retained earnings of the company. On the side of simplicity, the merit of reducing a large intangible value into smaller and more measurable terms would also seem to have appeal.

On the assumption that it would perhaps be difficult for the average shareholder to relate to a measure of value in a report of aggregate earnings totaling in the hundreds of thousands or millions of dollars, the reduction of this total to a simple small number of dollars and cents per share would appear not only to simplify the report but also to put it in terms more readily understood. In fact, the apparent virtue of this simplified way of reporting earnings has led directly into attempts on the part of the shareholder and others to then place a qualitative value on what is no more than a quantitative measurement. In what is perhaps a classic *non-sequitur* in the financial evaluation of the profit measurement, the investor—and at times the management of the company —then proceeds to make a value judgment concerning what he believes to be the profitability of the earnings per share report.

[87]

The Price/Earnings Ratio

For the listed security, the current market price of a share of common stock is divided by the reported earnings per share for the year and the resultant relationship is then expressed as the price/earnings (P/E) ratio. If, for example, a share of common is currently quoted at a price of $10.00 against a report of earnings amounting to $1.00 per share for the year, the multiple of earnings, or price/earnings ratio, is calculated at 10:1, meaning that the investing public had capitalized current earnings at a rate of 10%, paying $10.00 for each $1.00 of reported earnings. While the mechanics of the calculation are thus quite simple, the interpretation subsequently placed on the meaning of the P/E ratio is not.

To many so-called investors, the price/earnings ratio is frequently viewed as a value measurement in terms of rate of return, a measurement which is given qualitative values when compared to alternate investment opportunities. At a P/E ratio of 10:1, the investor is earning a 10% return on current market value and is prone to compare this directly with rates of return available on bank deposits, government securities, or corporate bonds. In doing so, he is thus making an assumption of equal risk in each investment as an unwitting part of his calculation by comparing the return on what is usually a partial participation in equity with a total participation in debt securities. He has thus left unanswered the question of what the rate of return on the common ought to be—that is, how much the earnings per share should be—as adequate compensation for the risk involved. He may indeed find the reported earnings rate "attractive" in relation to the quoted price and decide to invest more heavily, with the expectation that the market price will increase even further. And his judgment may also be seconded by the top management of his company, whose profit goals and objectives are centered around the Earnings per Share measurement and whose operating decisions are geared to an annual rate of increase in the figures reported.

Both the investor and the management may then become confused and dismayed a year later when the earnings report reaches a new high of $1.10 per share, only to find that an unresponsive market has dropped its evaluation to a P/E ratio of perhaps 8:1 for a price of $8.80 a share, a falloff of some 12% in market value while "earnings" were apparently going up nicely at a 10% annual rate of increase. Both have been misled in the use of the Earnings per Share measurement—the investor in using it as a value measurement in calculating a rate of return on his investment, and corporate management in its implied use of the P/E ratio as a measurement of the cost of equity capital in the marketplace. Both, in this instance, have been guilty of mistaking a *vehicle* for a measurement.

To put both the Earnings per Share measurement and its companion P/E ratio in proper perspective, it is necessary to take a look at the fundamental objectives of the truly informed investor whose judgment will ultimately prevail in the market. To do this, it is necessary to recognize the inexorable workings of the risk/reward relationship present in any investment decision.

Investor Expectations

Basically, the informed investor is willing to put his own capital out at risk in the expectation of suitable reward. If his expectations are ultimately realized, the risk will have been justified. If they are not, his subsequent evaluation of risk will be raised and his required rate of return increased. This principle of the dynamics of the capital market is often most evident in the constant fluctuation of the price/earnings multiple, a ratio which when properly used becomes no more than a *vehicle* for determining relative values. In using it simply as a vehicle, *the P/E ratio then merely measures the risk rate at which the investor is willing to capitalize current earnings*. In this process several value judgments are made, judgments which typically involve the use of at least two of the profit measurements already described.

The first and fundamental value judgment made by an informed investor is the total rate of Return on Invested Capital, the economic measurement of profitability of the enterprise itself. Since this also contains a built-in standard of comparison, the evaluation of return on capital then first determines the true level of profitability in which the investor is participating. If, for example, the current or projected rate of return is seen to be below the minimum acceptable level of 10%, the entire risk of the business is high and his participating investment in the equity perhaps even higher in risk. Next, since the average company will be employing at least a moderate amount of debt capital, and since the particular company in question may in fact be highly "leveraged" with debt, the informed investor will also carefully measure both the present and projected rates of return on equity, since as a shareholder he will be participating only in the equity earnings of the company. And, as has been seen, the adequacy of the Return on Equity measurement of profit is a direct function of the adequacy of the Return on Capital measurement itself, with the corresponding need for return on equity bearing a linear relationship to the amount of debt capital used in the business. In like fashion, the adequacy or fundamental value of the Earnings per Share measurement now becomes dependent upon the evaluation of return on equity, putting the earnings per share concept as a sort of third link in a chain of measurements if it is to be used properly. And when used properly, it becomes the vehicle for the price/

earnings ratio, a process in which the true *quality* of earnings can be quantified in terms of a desired rate of return. This process of reasoning assumed on the part of the investor is validated over the longer term by the single fact that companies with a high rate of return on total capital command higher price/earnings ratios than do companies with lower rates of return.

The relationship of market price to earnings is thus a fundamental one over the longer term, but is frequently one which is badly misunderstood by many corporate managers in the shorter term. Since the price/earnings ratio is expressed as a multiple of *current earnings*, a multiple of 5:1 would suggest a demand for a 20% rate of return; a multiple of 10:1, a 10% return; 20:1, a 5% return, and so forth. In fact, applying this measurement solely to current earnings, and thus failing to understand the basic implications of the process, has led some corporate managements *to equate such rates with the cost of equity capital*, and to assume—as in the case of one publicly held company whose shares had soared to a market value of 100 times earnings—that "we are financing our key assets . . . for next to nothing." The only logical extension of such beliefs would then also be to assume, since it would clearly follow, that the investor wanted virtually no return on his money, that he was quite willing to provide a permanent source of free capital to the business.

Such a proposition obviously defies common sense. The investor not only expects and will ultimately demand an adequate rate of return on his investment, but by paying a premium for the current level of earnings, *has already placed on management an even greater demand for a rapid gain in earnings in the future.* Far from having no cost to pay for the use of equity capital, the ultimate cost has already been identified in terms of the higher earnings the company is now expected to produce, the profit requirement for the future. In other words, the investor is not paying for present earnings but for the expectation of future earnings. Using both the past and the present as a base from which he projects his own estimate of the future, he pays what amounts to a premium for the right to participate in future earnings. This process of "discounting the future" is perhaps more readily seen in Figure 5, which assumes for purposes of demonstration that the investor has determined that a future net 10% rate of return is acceptable for his investment participation. His judgment of the price/earnings ratio necessary, to reach this goal is thus aimed at this financial "center of gravity" in making his pricing decision.

If, in this example, the investor is willing to pay $30.00 a share for common which is currently earning $1.00 a share, he is quite obviously not indicating a requirement for a return of something on the order of 3.0% which the price/earnings ratio of 30:1 would suggest. He is, in-

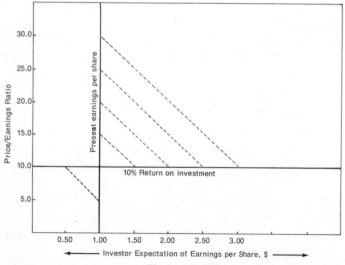

Figure 5

stead, expressing his opinion that the earnings per share will quickly increase to $3.00 a share, a level which will then yield a targeted rate of return of 10.0% on his investment. His projection of future earnings also assumes a continuation of improved earnings beyond the $3.00 per share level, an attainment which would then average out to a still higher rate of return over a longer period of time. He is also assuming, indirectly, that other investors will share his own view of future earnings prospects and will thus sustain a high multiple in the market should he elect to sell before the goal has been reached. If his judgment is correct he will then gain in either direction and receive a suitable compensation for the risk assumed. If his judgment proves to be wrong, as is frequently the case in high multiples of the P/E ratio, the ratio itself would then fall and fall sharply as a new set of assumptions moved into position. And as it falls, it provides along the way a clear demonstration to corporate management that it is by no means "financing its key assets for next to nothing." Its cost of equity capital had already been determined by the expectation of future earnings. Failure to reach the expected goal and the consequent sharp drop in the P/E ratio simply brings the demand for a current rate of return to the investor more nearly into line with the underlying cost of equity capital which must be met by management.

While the foregoing analysis is by no means proposed as any form of an exact science or mathematical formula by which the cost of equity capital can be determined over the short term, it does suggest a fundamental relationship between risk and return over the longer term. Taken in this perspective, the qualitative value placed upon the Earnings per Share measurement will be seen as an ultimate evaluation of total earnings measured against total capital employed. The visibility of such a relationship is, of course, limited to those companies whose shares are publicly traded, where a ready market exists for the exchange of share capital between investors. Once tested under these conditions, however, it will become apparent that the principle has broad application and that the risk/reward relationship evident in the marketplace works with equal force and logic in the use of all capital, public or private. It will serve to demonstrate, in short, that no business can be said to be exempt from the profit requirement, that the basic requirement for profit is measured in terms of the rate of return on invested capital, and that the earnings per share evaluation is not in itself a measure of profitability, although it is designed to look like one.

Why Earnings per Share Is Used

The question as to why the Earnings per Share measurement is used at all—let alone so widely used by so many large companies—would seem to be a natural one, since its use is clearly not as simple nor as uncomplicated as it might first appear. Its usefulness might also be questioned on the grounds of the degree of financial sophistication apparently required to place the measurement in adequate perspective. In spite of this, however, evidence suggests that it has been, and still is, rather widely used for several reasons. First, it has become an established and perhaps traditional way of reporting profits and has thus been embraced and carried forward by tradition alone. Secondly, it is easy to compute and gives the appearance both of simplicity and validity as a complete measurement of earnings for the equity investor. Third, and perhaps most importantly of all, *it is a measurement which will look good and which will continue to show apparent gains over an extended period of time even when the true profitability of the business is declining rather sharply.*

The apparent gain recorded by the Earnings per Share

measurement can first be illustrated by again using the figures for The Average Manufacturing Company (Chapter 1), whose results have already been analyzed in several different ways. In doing so, it might be well to summarize the various profit measurements applied to this very typical set of financial results for a manufacturing business and to demonstrate the apparent impact of each of the several ways of measuring profit. In summary, these measurements would show the following comparison of earnings results as compared with performance for the prior year:

	Current Year	Prior Year	Increase (Decrease)
Return on Invested Capital	10.0%	10.0%	—
Return on Assets	7.1%	8.0%	(11.0)%
Return on Equity	11.8%	11.3%	4.0%
Earnings per Share	$1.41	$1.24	13.0%

The earnings per share are, of course, arrived at in this example by dividing the net accounted earnings previously given for each of the two years as $1,410.00 and $1,240.00, respectively, by the constant number of 1,000 shares of common stock issued and outstanding. In retrospect, each of the four measurements of earnings has been drawn from the same set of financial reports, and each measurement in turn has suggested a different meaning or evaluation of results. In drawing out the last of these several measurements, it may perhaps become apparent why Earnings per Share has remained so popular as a reporting device for profit measurement. In this instance it indicates a solid gain of approximately 13% in earnings over the prior year *when in fact no gain at all actually took place.*

As has been shown, the rate of return on invested capital, the only complete measurement of economic productivity, remained completely unchanged at a constant

10% return. The dollars of earnings increased, but so did the amount of capital required to produce the earnings. The increase of $1,000 in debt capital served to "leverage" the return on equity about 4%, from a rate of 11.3% to 11.8%, but left the profitability of the equity investment unchanged as the risk rose in direct proportion to the increase in the use of debt.

In similar fashion, the quality of the Earnings per Share measurement was also affected to the same degree of higher risk as evidenced in the required increase in the rate of return on equity. And at the same time, the Earnings per Share measurement was also subjected to a second change, the increase of an additional $1,000 in the level of equity capital employed in the second year. In other words, *the earnings per share should have gone up simply because there was more money at work to produce the earnings.* The apparent gain of some 13% from $1.24 to $1.41 per share was, in fact, no gain at all but a constant level of performance when measured against the level of investment required to do the job.

Such reasoning is by no means obscure or beyond the awareness of the average investor if viewed in a somewhat different situation. If the Earnings per Share concept were to be applied to interest rates on a savings bank deposit, the similarity might become abundantly clear if the picture shown in Table 9 were assumed.

In this example, all interest earned is left on deposit at compound interest and the annual report of interest earned is likened to the Earnings per Share measurement. The report of interest earned shows an increase in every single year—comparable to the per share type of profit measurement—in spite of the fact that the bank has reduced its interest rate year by year over the ten-year period. No depositor, of course, would reason that he had earned $6.15 "per share" on the original $100.00 deposit,

Table 9

Year	Balance on Deposit, $	Interest Rate, %	Interest Earned, $
1	100.00	5.0	5.00
2	105.00	4.9	5.15
3	110.15	4.8	5.29
4	115.44	4.7	5.43
5	120.87	4.6	5.56
6	126.43	4.5	5.69
7	132.12	4.4	5.81
8	137.93	4.3	5.93
9	143.86	4.2	6.04
10	149.90	4.1	6.15

but on the current balance of $149.90, and would be well aware of the declining interest rates over the ten-year period. This same investor, however, does not for some reason carry this logic over into the measurements he applies to equity investment and frequently appears content with an apparent growth of earnings as suggested by the Earnings per Share measurement in spite of frequent reductions in the rate of profitability on his investment.

The earnings record of Eastman Kodak Company is a case in point. One of the strongest of the so-called blue chips, it is undoubtedly a highly profitable, solid, and well-managed company. But it, like so many other large publicly owned corporations, highlights its earnings in its published annual reports on the basis of earnings per share. By its own reporting, the record from 1966 to 1972 showed the following substantial increases year by year in earnings per share growth:

1966	$2.15	1970	$2.50
1967	2.19	1971	2.60
1968	2.33	1972	3.39
1969	2.49		

[97]

This reporting shows an apparent record of sustained earnings growth, with reported per share results climbing each year from $2.15 to $3.39 over a seven-year period. If taken at face value, it portrays a steady if moderate growth in the profitability of the company. The fact that this measurement was not taken at face value by the entire investment community, however, is found in the comments of one financial analyst writing in *The Wall Street Journal* on January 18, 1972, who stated in part that, "the company's earnings . . . are viewed by several analysts as downright disappointing since 1966," and that, "without the Kodak name as a crutch, the stock would probably be, deservedly, about 20 points lower." The reasoning behind such a judgment is to be found not in the record of earnings per share, but in the more fundamental measurement of the record of return on invested capital over the same period of time, a record (Table 10) which is in sharp contrast with the apparent gains suggested by the per share results.

When coupled with the overall measurement of the economic earning power of capital employed, the trend suggested by the earnings per share record takes on an entirely different meaning. From 1966 to 1971, per share earnings increased by 45 cents for a percentage gain of

Table 10

Year	Earnings per Share, $	Approximate Rate of Return on Capital, %
1966	2.15	25.4
1967	2.19	22.7
1968	2.33	21.6
1969	2.49	20.7
1970	2.50	18.9
1971	2.60	18.0
1972	3.39	21.1

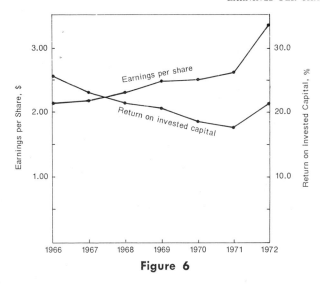

Figure 6

a little over 20%, while the true profitability of the company fell from a 25.4% rate of return on capital to 18.0%, *a decrease of nearly 30% in earnings.* Not until the per share results increased dramatically in 1972 did the total earnings begin to turn around and show a net gain over the prior year in terms of the rate of return on total capital employed. The divergence of these two measurements—both based on the same set of financial statements—is perhaps best illustrated in Figure 6, which clearly depicts the opposite trends indicated by each of these two measurements of profit.

Evaluation of Earnings per Share

Since the Earnings per Share measurement is widely used and is not likely to be discarded in the foreseeable future, its impact both on the investor and on corporate management must be dealt with. By itself it is, as has been shown, a highly misleading index of profitability. It serves, however, as a useful vehicle for price/earnings evaluations,

[99]

once it is linked to a more basic measurement of results.

Several attempts have been made to adjust the per share mathematics to some form of a value judgment or qualitative type of evaluation. One of the more notable attempts has been suggested by the institutional research firm of Faulkner, Dawkins & Sullivan, which emphasizes a rate of return approach to evaluating companies. Stating that "the price/earnings multiple just isn't adequate" and that "we've all been trapped in the catchwords of the business—a 10 P/E is cheap, 20 is full, 30 expensive. It's all nonsense," the firm suggests a new approach. It defines rate of return as the *earnings per share divided by the book value of the stock*, on the theory that "a company that can sustain a high return on equity will compound its earnings growth if a big chunk of earnings is reinvested." This approach plainly suggests the need to link per share earnings with fundamental profitability, a change which might also be accomplished by converting *earnings* per share into a measurement of *profitability* per share, thus introducing a qualitative aspect to the per share report.

The technique might be to start with an earnings per share figure which represented an acceptable earnings base—such as the 1966 results for Eastman Kodak when $2.15 a share reflected a net 25.4% return on total capital—and then to adjust the per share results in following periods to correspond with changes in the overall rate of return. Using this technique, the *profitability per share* for Kodak over the same seven-year period previously given would then be as shown in Figure 7.

On this basis, the apparent gain in earnings from $2.15 a share in 1966 to $3.39 a share in 1972 is given a new perspective. The $3.39 reported in 1972 is worth only $1.83 in terms of earning power, reflecting the same rate of decline as the rate of return on capital which started at 25.4% and which ended the period at 21.1%.

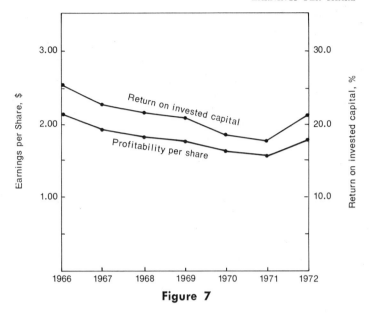

Figure 7

A Balanced Look at Profits

The several measurements of profit which have been examined—ranging all the way from the basic rate of return
on invested capital to the vehicle of earnings per share—
present a random definition of profit which can serve
only to confuse and mislead both management and the
investor unless the measurements are somehow balanced
and given perspective. The need to do so is urgent. In
reporting its earnings for the first quarter of 1974, American Telephone reported its *dollars of earnings* as $799.4
million, up 14% from the first quarter of 1973, with
earnings per share of $1.33, up 12% from the $1.19 reported a year earlier. The only link to the level of profitability was then contained in the statement that the earnings represented "the highest rate of return on invested
capital—8.56%—since 1929." In using three different
measurements of profit in one report the company is ap-

[101]

parently striving to show substantially improved results for the period, but the random use of such measurements does little to measure the current trend of earnings or to inform the investor of the true rate of gain in profitability over the 1973 period.

A more useful approach in reporting its earnings was taken by Alcoa during the last two years. In reporting the first quarter results for 1973, John D. Harper, chairman and chief executive of the company, added a disclaimer to the increase in per share results by stating that earnings were "well short of our goals and short of the long-term requirements of the company," adding that "a continued low return on capital employed surely would limit our future." This emphasis on basic profitability apparently paid off. In reporting first-quarter results for 1974, a year later, Mr. Harper noted that the return on invested capital had increased from 3.7% to 7.8% during the year, but stressed that "based on present conditions we need a 10.0% return" in the current year.

Such reporting is both refreshing and reassuring and points the way toward a balanced view of profits, one which will add substance to the numbers and a qualitative interpretation of results. In his book *Earnings per Share and Management Decisions*, John Childs says of profit goals that, "the place to start is with the return on long term capital." * Such a starting point is long overdue, and those managements which grasp its value will do much in the way of adding some earnings sense to the present confused picture of profit reporting.

* Englewood Cliffs, N.J. Prentice-Hall, 1971.

seven

The effect
of
hidden capital

THE VARIOUS MEASUREMENTS OF PROFIT described in
previous chapters have shown the need for a basic
evaluation of earnings in terms of the rate of return
on invested capital. Since capital provides the financial base for all earnings, it is thus obvious that the
earnings arising from the use of capital must be related back to the same base which produced them.
And to properly measure and evaluate the rate of
return, it has further been shown that the calculation should measure *the total stream of earnings
against the total value of capital employed* in the

business. In actual practice, however, only a small minority of even those companies using the return on capital concept of profit measurement are properly evaluating earnings or adequately setting profit goals and objectives for the future. For many, if indeed not for most, the measurement is rendered invalid by the presence of hidden capital.

As has been shown, the profit measurement of return on equity falls short of a valid evaluation of earnings performance, since by its very nature it fails to take into account the economic use of the "hidden" debt capital. By assessing only the interest cost on debt—and thus exempting it from the higher cost of risk capital employed in the business—the return on equity is inflated by the level of debt used. In this sense it compresses the bulk of the reported earnings to a smaller base, a base representing only part of the capital actually used to run the business. And by the same token, the process of inflating the rate of return and of thus overstating the overall profitability of the enterprise is also present in many reports of the rate of return on invested capital. It is present when neither the total value of capital employed nor the total earnings produced by that capital are fully recognized in the calculation. To the extent that such hidden capital exists in a company, the planning, budgeting, controlling, and entire decision-making process may indeed be heading down a dangerous path.

The Effect of Leasing

One of the principal sources of hidden capital, if indeed not the largest in business today, is the capital provided in the form of leased assets. Although the full extent of current industrial leasing is perhaps not known, several sources estimated it as a $10 billion dollar business as far back as 1969, with computer leasing at that time accounting for some $5 billion of the total while vehicle leasing for cars and trucks was placed in excess of $3 billion annually. The trend has certainly spread, climbing to a reported $60 billion total by 1972, and today embraces a wide segment of industrial assets ranging from land and buildings to machinery, tools, and equipment. It has many obvious attractions. On the plus side, it offers a strong hedge against obsolescence.

In referring to computer leasing alone, one publication noted that "design changes, technological advances, etc. in EDP equipment alone creates new models with greater capabilities and provides almost instant obsolescence." Leasing thus provides a flexibility of moving in and out of equipment at far less risk than outright purchase. Secondly, it offers certain tax advantages as opposed to ownership in the form of more rapid expense write-offs against taxable income, although this latter advantage has been sharply curtailed with respect to leases which are in effect no more than conditional sales contracts. And third, it has the obvious advantage of providing a source of assets not otherwise available to companies with limited working capital. Leasing thus has a useful role to play in business and a proper place in the financial management of capital employed.

It also has an improper usage and plays a very misleading role in many instances. As one writer put it, "*a cleaner balance sheet* has also been cited as an advantage of leasing. That is, if a company borrows the money to buy an asset, the debt appears on its balance sheet. If the asset was acquired under a lease, the obligation will appear only in a footnote and sometimes not even there. Thus, it was said, a company would be able to get more leverage . . . because the 'true' debt structure of a company may be concealed." This rather candid appraisal of motives strikes directly at the heart of the matter and exposes the subterfuge that many companies have adopted in an attempt to keep this type of debt financing "off the balance sheet." While both the SEC and the Accounting Principles Board have taken steps to require the capitalization of certain noncancellable lease contracts, much of leasing still remains hidden from view and unaccounted for in financial reporting.

Leasing is, very plainly, a form of debt, and quite often the most expensive form of debt available. As one manager put it, "we leased equipment because we didn't have and couldn't get the working capital." It is thus not only debt, but at times also a debt of last resort, a source of borrowed funds when no other sources are available.

Regardless of the reasons for leasing, however, *the impact* of leasing needs to be recognized in the financial statements of the company and its consequences given full measure in the report of earnings. Since leasing is a form of debt, it ought to be treated as debt, and this means full recognition on the balance sheet as a capitalized lease-obligation. And since the capitalization of leased capital would require an offsetting entry on the asset side of the ledger, the process would insure a complete evaluation of both the total value of assets and the total value of capital actually employed in the business. Such full recording is mandatory if profit measurements are to make any sense, and while the process may be unpalatable to those managements who have plainly been trying to keep such information away from the balance sheet, the impact and the need for such disclosure is by no means lost on the accounting profession itself.

In an interview in the March 15, 1973, issue of *Forbes Magazine*, Harvey Kapnick, chairman of the accounting firm of Arthur Andersen & Company, had this to say on the subject of leasing:

Company reports . . . don't tell an investor what he wants to know—what his company has got that is valuable to him in producing a stream of earnings. On the liability side I would put *all* commitments: Many leases, for instance, create more obligations than debt instruments. I would get to a financial statement with no intangibles, because intangibles have no value apart from the operation. You would then have a financial statement with nothing but economic values and liabilities.

The same concern has also been echoed by the financial press. In its edition of May 15, 1972, the *New York Post* referred to a growing awareness of the impact of leasing in an article entitled "Leases For Burying Debt," in which it stated in part that, "the attempt through lease financing to conceal a company's financial obligation has concerned a number of observers." Including, apparently, a spokesman for Moody's Investor Services, who is quoted further on in the article as saying "It's an attempt by companies to circumvent their balance sheet. They may already be up against their borrowing limit."

While the need to do something about the impact of leasing is thus finding a voice in many informed bodies of opinion, little is being done about it in practice. And although the need may be complex, a workable solution to the problem is not, and is available to any financial manager seeking a viable measurement for profit management.

Valuing Leased Capital

Since the need with respect to leased capital is to determine and measure the value of capital employed from this source, the problem of valuation narrows down very simply to one of technique. At least three methods are available. The first, and also the most expensive, is to have an appraisal of present value made by an appraisal expert. While this takes both time and money, it may well be worth the investment in determining the value of a multiplicity of leases covering several types of assets employed. A second method is the use of tables which classify various categories of equipment and give a percentage adjustment to be applied, based on the age or year of acquisition in order to update the original cost to at least approximate current replacement value. This method is certainly less expensive and probably of sufficient accuracy as regards the valuation of standard types of equipment. The third method is simply that of making your own best estimate based on rule of reason and some informed judgment. It has, perhaps, particular application in estimating values for land and buildings, an area where leasing is most common for many companies.

As an example of this latter technique it might be useful to consider the situation of a typical manufacturing business which leases some five acres of land and a building with 100,000 square feet of space in an industrial park. Although the lease commitment is shown as a footnote in the audit report, the only measurable impact of the leasing in the financial statements is the recording of the annual lease payments of $200,000 as reflected on the Income Statement. In condensed form, the financial results for the year are presented in the Income Statement and Balance Sheet, Exhibits C and D.

The 18.5% net rate of return reported on invested capital is deemed highly satisfactory, and operating plans for the future include no major changes in pricing levels, cost control, or asset management. The results, in short, appear to be quite profitable, and the financial elements of the business are thought to be adequately balanced.

A further look at the relationship between the turnover rate of the reported capital and the reported earnings percent to sales, however, reveals that the apparently high rate of an 18.5% return on capital is supported by

Exhibit C

INCOME STATEMENT	
Sales	$10,000,000
Direct Cost of Sales	4,000,000
Gross Margin	6,000,000
Period Expenses	
Lease Cost	200,000
All Other	4,800,000
Total	5,000,000
Pretax Profit	1,000,000
Provision for Income Tax	500,000
Net Earnings After Taxes	$ 500,000

an abnormally high turnover of capital for a manufacturing business, as disclosed by the analysis in Table 11.

In other words, the annual turnover rate of 3.7 times for reported capital is considerably higher than should be expected, and in fact is more indicative of the ratio of

Exhibit D

BALANCE SHEET	
Cash	$ 250,000
Accounts Receivable	1,250,000
Inventory	1,650,000
Property and Plant	600,000
Miscellaneous Assets	300,000
Total Assets	$4,050,000
Operating Debt	(1,350,000)
Invested Capital	$2,700,000

Reported Earnings

$$\frac{\text{Net Earnings}}{\text{Capital}} \quad \frac{\$ \ 500,000}{\$2,700,000} = 18.5\% \text{ return on capital}$$

Table 11

	Turnover Rate	
	As Reported	Normal Rate
Cash	40.0	40.0
Receivables	8.0	8.0
Inventory	6.0	6.0
Property and Plant	16.7	4.0
Total Assets	2.5	1.7
Operating Debt	(7.5)	(7.5)
Invested Capital	3.7	2.0

capital to sales to be found in a retailing business than in manufacturing. And since all other turnover rates appear to be normal, the high turnover of total capital is quickly identified in the low level of investment of only $600,000 charged to the Property and Plant account, an amount which in fact covers only the machinery, equipment, and furniture and fixtures which the company has purchased and shown as an asset on the balance sheet. By comparison, a normal turnover rate of 4.0 times would indicate the probable use of some $2.5 million in the total fixed assets of the business, suggesting the presence of a possible $1.9 million in "hidden" capital.

This approximation can then be tested by an analysis of the estimated value of the leased assets employed, an analysis where judgment might indicate the following:

Assumed Asset Value
Land: 5 acres @ $30,000/acre	$ 150,000
Building: 100,000 sq. ft. @ $17.50	1,750,000
Total Assumed Value	$1,900,000

As a further test of this value, it must next be recognized that the total lease payments for the property contain two basic elements of cost: the depreciation of the asset and the interest equivalent for the use of money. A breakout of these two elements contained in the total lease expense of $200,000 paid for the year might then be assumed as shown in Table 12.

If the second analysis then tends to substantiate the first, the financial results as reported for the year should then be adjusted for the effect of the leased or hidden capital. The first step is to add the value assumed for the leased assets to the book value of capital as reflected on the Balance Sheet, restructuring the statement of capital employed as though the leased values had in fact been capitalized in the accounting process:

Book Capital	$2,700,000
Leased Capital	1,900,000
Total Capital Employed	$4,600,000

Secondly, since the leased capital thus derived is a form of debt, the interest cost of the debt must next be added back to the accounted earnings to determine the total stream of earnings produced by the total capital employed. In this step, the books are being adjusted to show the transactions which would have taken place if in fact

Table 12

Estimated Value of Building	$1,750,000
Depreciable Life	25 years
Depreciation @ 4.0% per year	$ 70,000
Total Lease Expense	$ 200,000
Estimated Depreciation	70,000
Net Interest Equivalent	$ 130,000

$$\frac{\text{Assumed Interest} \qquad \$\ 130,000}{\text{Assumed Asset Value} \qquad \$1,900,000} = \text{Approximately 7.0\% per year}$$

the funds had been borrowed in the form of direct debt and the proceeds used to purchase the asset. In doing so, the interest portion of the lease cost is added back to accounted earnings and the remainder, the depreciation portion, is left as a charge against earnings:

Net Accounted Earnings	$500,000
After-Tax Interest Cost	65,000
Total Stream of Earnings	$565,000

As adjusted, the total stream of earnings of $565,000 measured against the total capital employed of $4,600,000 would show a rate of return of only 12.3% on invested capital, considerably below the level of 18.5% the company had thought it was earning. And with the lower assessment of earnings, it is perhaps safe to assume that the management processes of planning, budgeting, and controlling will take on a somewhat different aspect for the company in the future.

The Effect of Undervalued Assets

A second source of hidden capital will frequently be found in the valuation of assets that are owned and which are reflected on the company books. Current accounting practice still dictates that these assets be valued on the Balance Sheet at the lower of cost or market, thus typically reflecting *acquisition cost less depreciation* rather than current value, a practice that has long since outlived its concept. Its present effect has been to *seriously undervalue many of the assets of the business,* and hence to understate the value of total capital employed.

Until recent years, the problem has admittedly been a minor one for the average company. It has been minor because the overall valuation of assets reflected at least a close approximation of current value, with the fixed assets of land, buildings, and equipment in particular being either of fairly recent acquisition or through the continual renewal of such assets by the reinvestment of the funds generated by depreciation charges. Until recently, in fact, the problem of asset undervaluation arising from age alone has been confined to the older industries such as textiles and railroads, where the original acquisition of assets still in use may date back for fifty years or more. In these situations, it has not been uncommon to find such major productive assets as buildings or equipment either fully depreciated or carried on the books at a nominal value while still producing the mainstream of the company's earnings. Or to find land values stated at original cost as opposed to current market values which are perhaps several millions of dollars in excess of the book figures. In these cases, the need to restate the assets at current replacement value has been present for a long time. It has generally been neglected and has had serious consequences for the profit management of companies who were in this position.

The problem of undervaluation of the Balance Sheet, however, is no longer confined to these older industries or limited to those situations involving only the extreme age of assets acquired. It is currently widespread and is affecting all companies, and seriously so, due to the impact of the present rate of inflation in the economy. It is posing a major problem not only in the field of accounting, a field where change is long overdue, but consequently in the field of financial management of the business, a field which has been geared too closely to accounted results.

In the face of what is now generally referred to as "double digit" inflation, the current replacement value of assets and capital is quickly hidden from view by the accounting process, with book values becoming obsolete almost as soon as they are recorded. For the truth of inflation is that its effect is not confined by any means to the operating side of the business where rising costs for labor, materials, and supplies are quickly identified and to a large extent compensated for in rising prices. The hidden effect of inflation is far more serious and apparently far more difficult to manage in that *it also results in a rapid erosion of capital.*

Inflation, even at its present level, does not, obviously, have any serious or measurable impact on the average use of capital in the form of cash or receivables. These so-called quick assets of a business can be thought of as riding with inflation and as therefore being stated at all times at "current value." The problem first appears in the inventory account, particularly where the LIFO (last-in-first-out) method of inventory valuation is used. For while this method does serve to avoid inflated "inventory profits" as well as the subsequent payment of higher income taxes on such reported profits, the effect on the Balance Sheet is to siphon off the most recent—and inflated—costs of the inventory acquired and to leave the earlier costs as the basis for valuation. This process thus reflects an asset stated at values which can no longer be duplicated, values perhaps far below the current and constantly rising replacement cost of the inventory on hand.

In a large sense, however, the impact of inflation on inventory values is of less consequence in most companies than is the impact on the fixed asset accounts, which usually represent a larger portion of the total capital employed. Inventories, eventually, will move up in asset value as inflation continues, while in many instances the valuation of land, buildings, machinery, and equipment will be left far behind. With average depreciation rates running at something close to 10% for the book valuation of equipment, values are written down quite rapidly while an inflation rate in excess of 10% is pushing the replacement cost up, thus quickly compounding the divergence of values within a short span of time. In several Latin American countries where inflation has been running at a rate of 50% a year or higher, many firms have found it necessary to revalue their assets at the close of each month in order to plan for operations in the ensuing 30 days. With a hopefully more moderate rate of inflation, business in the United States is currently facing a probable need to do the same thing, at least on an annual basis.

The need will be for a constant updating of values, which must encompass both the assets leased as well as the assets owned. And in the process, the question will naturally arise as to how to then depreciate the higher appraised values in order to reflect a proper charge for the cost of such "wasting assets" against the income for the period. Until such time as the tax laws are changed to recognize this need—that is, to eliminate what is currently an effective tax on capital itself—the only guidelines possible are those of best judgment.

Impact on Profit Management

In the meantime, the impact on profit and profit management can be severe for those companies who fail to take action. The March 1974 issue of *Fortune* magazine identified the point quite clearly in an article entitled "Profits Aren't As Good As They Look" in which current reported profits were shown to "include illusory gains that show up on the books only because depreciation does not cover the rising costs of replacing used-up machinery." The situation of undervalued assets is thus coupled with a parallel situation of understated costs, both of which lead to a compounding of illusory profits. The net effect is not only the erosion of both earnings and capital, but the eventual erosion of business survival.

Of the two sides of this coin, the effect of inflation on operating costs is more readily identifiable and more prone to corrective action. Once freed from price controls, most companies have taken steps to pass on these higher costs in the form of higher prices, prices which of course tend to feed inflation itself and to return full circle in still higher costs for labor, materials, and supplies. Such price increases are both after the fact and usually insufficient in that they will require upward adjustment again almost immediately to meet the next and apparently inexorable round of cost increases about to come. Other companies are going beyond the "catch up" phase of meeting inflation and are going to great lengths to project future costs, to restructure product lines, to reduce distribution costs and discounts, and to effect further cost reductions as an alternative to still further increases in the selling price of the product. It is a continuous task and much is being done at a considerable expenditure of both time and effort.

Unfortunately, much of this effort will be wasted. In attempts to overcome the erosion of *accounted* profits, management may ultimately lose the battle for *economic profit* unless the full impact of "hidden" capital is taken into account in its profit planning. No "profit" can be said to exist for any business until all costs have been recovered. And this very clearly includes the cost of all capital employed, a cost whose recovery will add earnings sense to the profit dollars reported.

eight

Profit measurement

of the

balance sheet

Since the subject of profit measurement carries with it the concept of *profit management*, the question of measurement cannot be confined to the Income Statement alone. Profitability, to be measured properly, depends upon the management of capital as well as on the management of operating income, and the management of capital depends in turn upon an ability to measure its use. That ability is typically not present when management is confronted with the usual accounting type of presentation to be found in the average Balance Sheet.

Of the two financial statements, the Balance Sheet is usually relegated to a poor second position at best, insofar as management attention is concerned, with the Income Statement becoming the apparent focal point for both measurement and decision making. Since it contains the more active accounts for sales, costs, and accounted profit, the Statement of Income is in fact regarded by most managements as the primary financial statement, with the Balance Sheet plainly secondary or subordinate to it. And for those managements presently using one of the partial measurements of profit already described, the transition to a full profit measurement in terms of the rate of return on invested capital may seem to be a major change in itself. If the use of such a profit measurement is to offer the opportunity for profit improvement, however, the concept of profitability must be extended to the Balance Sheet as well.

Many changes in financial reporting have been made over the years to make the typical Income Statement more understandable to the nonfinancial manager. The use of direct costing or marginal income analysis, for example, was a major departure in managerial accounting in that it presented for the first time a picture of the way a business actually functions. This, in turn, led the way to a direct measurement of profit contribution by product or product group, by class of sale, by sales region or territory, and by several other methods of analyzing operations. It made possible a quick determination of break-even point volume and set the stage for a more effective approach to pricing decisions and marketing strategies. Its full use has, in short, transformed the former accounting presentation of income and expense into a workable and understandable tool for management.

Nothing comparable has been done with respect to the Balance Sheet. It still stands, as it has for years, as a "statement of condition," a statement designed by accountants for use by bankers and often not fully understood by either. In its form of listing assets, for example, in the order of their liquidity, and by its use of a multitude of ratios showing the relationship of assets to liabilities, it gives the appearance of placing emphasis on the *accumulation* of capital rather than on its *utilization*. To the average manager, the information presented on the Balance Sheet seems remote from operations, not tied in with such results-oriented objectives as sales and reported earnings. At best, it offers a picture of ending balances from which a manager must draw some conclusions or interpretations if indeed he is expected to react to the statement at all. Typically, he has had difficulty enough in understanding the Income Statement in the past and is generally ill-equipped to cope with the more abstract picture of assets, liabilities, and net worth, elements whose very terms seem to be couched in a specialized language of their own.

Impact of the Balance Sheet

If he reads the statement at all, the average manager will feel compelled to at least try to find some meaning in it: His first reaction may be to try to sort out the "good" from the "bad." The leadoff item that will first meet his eye is the cash balance at the end of the period. And if a comparative Balance Sheet is issued, he may note that the cash balance has increased substantially over the prior period. He will hardly look upon this as a "bad" measurement, since he will liken it to his own personal view of cash, a situation where the acquisition of "more" has been found to be desirable. With regard to the balances shown for Accounts Receivable, he will probably have mixed emotions, or at best confusion, as to what may be "good" or "bad." If sales have gone up in the current period an increase in receivables will appear reassuring.

If, on the other hand, sales have remained fairly constant he may only dimly perceive a possible collection problem in the higher balance in this asset account. In any event, he will probably reason that this is someone else's problem and has nothing to do with current earnings or profitability.

On inventory, he is likely to have an entirely different reaction. Conditioned by repeated memos and warnings from the front office to "get the inventory down," he will see any increase in the inventory balance as "bad," without relating the figure to anything else. The fairly constant level of fixed assets, in turn, will have little meaning for him, nor will the several miscellaneous accounts for prepaid expenses and deferred charges. Neither will the right-hand side of the Balance Sheet offer much in the way of intelligence with its listing of debt and equity accounts, although he may tend to think of items classed as "reserves" as being some form of cash balances and thus become hopelessly lost in the maze of double-entry bookkeeping. In short, he will have been subjected to a document which is both abstract and confusing, a financial report which seems to be designed for someone else, a set of figures alien to his need and with little if any connecting link to his responsibility for operations.

If true, such an attitude is at least understandable. And it is by no means isolated to those members of middle and upper management who are so readily classified as "nonfinancial" managers—meaning, in essence, that they have had no formal training or indoctrination into the workings of the accounting or bookkeeping process. Very few members of "top" management, in fact very few chief executives, have any better understanding or more informed view of the Balance Sheet, either on how to read it or on what to do about it. And this lack of understanding throughout all levels of management has nothing to do with lack of initiative or indifference, but is directly due to the failure of the financial reporting process itself. As a *passive* sort of financial report, the Balance Sheet reports but does not truly inform, and reflects a "statement of condition" without any reference to what that condition ought to be. For unlike the Income Statement, the Balance Sheet is not action-oriented and contains no qualitative measurements or guide to corrective action required.

Again, the full impact of this condition can perhaps best be shown by a typical set of financial reports for a manufacturing business. To illustrate the lack of impact which the Balance Sheet has on profit management, an example will be used where the company is striving to measure profit in terms of the rate of return on invested capital, capital which can be assumed to be measured properly with respect to current value and which is fully stated with no unaccounted-for "hidden" assets (see Exhibit E).

In the example shown in Exhibit E sales for the current period have increased sharply for a full 15% gain in volume, a gain that has carried down to a corresponding increase in marginal income at a constant rate of 45% in gross margin on sales. To achieve this gain in volume and operating margin, the total period expenses of the business have further been controlled at an increase of only 8%, following the predictable need for a step-rate increase in operating overhead at this higher level of sales volume. The net result has carried down to a 40% gain in total net earnings, thus presenting a picture of a solid gain in both sales and earnings with more than adequate control over costs and expenses. However, when these net earnings are measured against the average capital employed, the *profitability* for the period is seen to have declined from a net 10.0% return on invested capital to 9.7%, a step backward in overall progress in spite of the

Exhibit E

INCOME STATEMENT	Current Period	Prior Period
Sales	$11,500	$10,000
Direct Cost of Goods Sold	6,300	5,500
Gross Margin	$ 5,200	$ 4,500
P/V Ratio	45%	45%
Period Expense	$ 3,800	$ 3,500
Income from Operations	1,400	1,000
Interest Expense	200	—
Pretax Profit	1,200	1,000
Provision for Income Taxes	600	500
Net Accounted Earnings	600	500
Add Net Interest Cost	100	—
Total Earnings	$ 700	$ 500
Average Invested Capital	$ 7,200	$ 5,000
Return on Invested Capital	9.7%	10.0%

operating gains reported. Capital, obviously, has increased even faster than the earnings. The typical accounting form of the Balance Sheet (Exhibit F), however, will do little to demonstrate this side of the equation, to provide any measurement of profitability in the use of capital.

When some of the traditional measurements are applied to the Balance Sheet, several "good" things appear to have happened. For one, the net working capital—the excess of "Current Assets over Current Liabilities—has increased from $2,500 to $2,700, an apparent move in the direction of a "stronger" Balance Sheet. Secondly, the so-called quick assets of cash and receivables have gone up by $1,000, denoting another apparent gain in the direction of liquidity. In the opposite direction, Accounts Payable has decreased by $400, evidencing a reduced level of current indebtedness to trade creditors, while the

Exhibit F

BALANCE SHEET		
	Current Balance	Prior Balance
Current Assets		
Cash	$ 400	$ 250
Accounts Receivable	2,100	1,250
Inventory	2,500	1,650
Prepaid Expenses	800	700
Total Current Assets	$5,800	$3,850
Fixed Assets		
Property and Plant, at cost	$4,100	$4,000
Less Reserve for Depreciation	1,600	1,500
Net Property and Plant	$2,500	$2,500
Total Assets	$8,300	$6,350
Current Liabilities		
Accounts Payable	$ 700	$1,100
Accrued Expenses	250	150
Accrued Taxes	150	100
Notes Payable	2,000	—
Total Current Liabilities	$3,100	$1,350
Net Worth		
Common Stock	$1,000	$1,000
Retained Earnings	4,200	4,000
Total Net Worth	$5,200	$5,000
Total Liabilities and Net Worth	$8,300	$6,350

Net Worth has shown a net increase of $200, which somehow seems to correspond with the higher net earnings for the period. The only jarring note would seem to be the presence of $2,000 in Notes Payable to the bank, a new account but one which is probably attributed to the "need to finance the higher volume" and given little further thought. All in all, the Balance Sheet seems solid and creates an impression of progress. Total assets have increased, net worth is up, and current payables are down —generalities which seem to support the progress as reported on the Income Statement itself. The accounting form of the Balance Sheet thus generates no area of concern, much less any sort of measurement of the profitability of capital employed. It presents, in short, no qualitative analysis, no statement of what the balances *should have been*, and thus no indication of any corrective action needed.

The net result of the two financial reports is to leave management confused as to what has happened and uncertain as to what, if anything, to do about it. A creditable job has been done in increasing both the sales and the earnings, but in spite of this the new measurement of profit which management has learned to apply—the Rate of Return on Invested Capital—has gone down. Something is clearly missing and additional information must be needed.

Balance Sheet Budgets

In facing a similar situation, many companies have sought an answer in preparing budgets for the Balance Sheet accounts, a technique which has worked well in planning and controlling the operating accounts. Such attempts, however, are generally confined to a projection or extrapolation of existing balances, an exercise which simply tries to predict the probable level of investment to be anticipated at some point in the future. This sort of "budgeting" has little to do with the *need for capital,* and even less with its subsequent impact on profitability.

If, for example, the company in question had budgeted sales at a level of $15,000 for the second period, an attempt to budget the Balance Sheet for the same period might have taken the form of Table 13.

In other words, a general approach to budgeting dollar levels on the Balance Sheet would take the form of increasing the allowance for cash, receivables, inventory, and prepaid expenses in direct proportion to the planned increase in sales, a reasonable assumption since the higher levels of investment would be needed in direct support of the higher volume. A different reasoning and different approach would then apply to the Fixed Assets accounts for land, buildings, and machinery where the amount budgeted would indicate a plan to reinvest only the current charges for depreciation for the period. Different reasoning would also typically apply to the budgeting of the Operating Debt accounts, the noninterest-bearing

Table 13

	First Period Actual	Second Period Budget
Sales Volume	$10,000	$15,000
Balance Sheet		
Cash	$ 250	$ 375
Accounts Receivable	1,250	1,875
Inventory	1,650	2,475
Fixed Assets	2,500	2,500
Prepaid Expenses	700	1,025
Total Assets	6,350	8,250
Operating Debt	(1,350)	(1,350)
Invested Capital	$5,000	$ 6,900

payables and accrued expenses. Since the impact on profitability and the consequent management of these accounts is seldom understood, a general assumption would be made that they would somehow remain at a constant level in the future.

If the sales budget of $15,000 were then achieved, the Balance Sheet budget would reflect a statement of what the various levels of asset investment should have been for the period, and consequently would indicate a measurable deviation from plan or a need for corrective action when the budgeted assets were compared with actual balances. The method would thus have merit if the sales for the ensuing period were also exactly on budget. The fact that the sales volume is seldom so predictable, however, next leads to a very serious misuse of this type of Balance Sheet budgeting, that of *comparing budgeted dollars to actual dollars of investment regardless of the level of sales volume attained.*

With actual sales of only $11,500, as shown on the operating statement for the period, the company might then proceed to compare the budgeted assets for the planned $15,000 in sales with the actual balances supporting $11,500 in volume as shown in Table 14.

The general picture presented by this sort of comparison of "budget to actual" in Table 14 is thus one of very close control over the total assets employed, with the excess investment in receivables offset by a reduction in prepaid expenses—leaving only a minor deviation in total. The larger variance in the level of capital employed will be seen in all likelihood as no more than the consequence of keeping the payables down, an apparently "good" measurement and not one indicative of any necessary corrective action. In short, aside from a brief notation that the collection of receivables might benefit from more attention, nothing is learned from the Balance Sheet presentation or comparison to budget which will

Table 14

	Budget	Actual	Variance
Cash	$ 375	$ 400	$ (25)
Accounts Receivable	1,875	2,100	(225)
Inventory	2,475	2,500	(25)
Fixed Assets	2,500	2,500	—
Prepaid Expenses	1,025	800	225
Total Assets	$8,250	$8,300	$ (50)
Operating Debt	(1,350)	(1,100)	(250)
Invested Capital	$6,900	$7,200	$(300)

enable the company to improve its job of capital management in the future. No connecting link with the current operating results has been established, and no index or other measurement of profitability has been suggested with regard to the Balance Sheet figures. It continues as a passive and somewhat disconnected type of financial statement which does little to serve management or to add to the measure of profit.

A New Type of Report

The Balance Sheet in its present accounted form is thus an outmoded document and one which requires substantial change in the manner of presentation if it is to serve as a useful tool for profit management. It can be done, and done rather simply, if the concept of "statement of condition" can be discarded, or supplemented, by a new type of report aimed at *the economic use of capital employed*. In other words, the concept of profit measurement can also be applied to the Balance Sheet if economic values are substituted for accounted balances.

To accomplish this change, capital—as well as the assets provided by capital—must be put into perspective as

[127]

an integral part of the measurement of profit. Since a complete measurement of profitability must take into account not only the total stream of earnings from operations but also the total value of the capital required to produce those earnings, the two sides of the equation are inseparable in fact and must be joined and made inseparable in reporting. And since the two are thus interdependent, it is obvious that the final measurement of profitability is dependent on a combination of the two elements which join to produce the final result. On the operating side, the measurement used is to state the net earnings as a percent of sales. On the investment side, the connecting link is expressed as the turnover rate of assets, liabilities, and capital—all related to the same dollar volume of sales as shown on the operating statement. The technique for a new or supplementary form of Balance Sheet reporting is thus to measure not the dollar balances against the dollars budgeted, but the turnover rates themselves, a technique which will then bring the Balance Sheet completely into phase with the Income Statemer. and replace bookkeeping procedures with a measure of profit management.

Such a report would measure *the use of capital* related to operations and report the dollar impact of the *management of capital*, a dollar impact which would constitute a profit type of measurement for the Balance Sheet itself. Assuming, for example, that the company in question had determined that the turnover rates in the first period were at normal levels and had therefore budgeted a continuing rate of turnover for the ensuing period, a "Use of Capital" report might then take the form shown as Exhibit G.

In computing the dollar impact of the management of capital, the *budgeted turnover rates are applied to the actual dollar volume of sales to determine the level of investment allowed for operations.* The dollar difference between allowable and actual investment is then shown

Exhibit G

USE OF CAPITAL REPORT			
	Turnover Rate		Better
	Budget	Actual	(Worse), $
Cash	40.0	28.6	(110)
Accounts Receivable	8.0	5.5	(660)
Inventory	6.0	4.6	(590)
Fixed Assets	4.0	4.8	470
Other Assets	14.3	14.3	—
Total Assets	1.6	1.4	(890)
Operating Debt	(7.4)	(11.5)	(550)
Capital Employed	2.0	1.6	(1,440)

in the right-hand column as "better or worse" than plan. In doing this, the report adds to the Balance Sheet, reporting a new qualitative dimension: *a measure of what the balances ought to be* for the use of capital to reach the profit target planned. It presents a far different picture, one which identifies immediately both the area for management attention as well as the amount of corrective action required. It adds the responsibility for the management of assets and capital to the responsibility for operating results as well as putting a new perspective on the meaning of the Balance Sheet values.

The increase in the cash balance, for example, is no longer seen as a desirable gain in liquidity, but as a layer of idle capital which must be put to work. The extent to which the collection of receivables has slowed down is now measured in terms of dollars, dollars of the company's capital being used by customers beyond the time calculated in the selling price of the product. Inventory management is no longer left with the vague dictum of "getting the inventory down" but has a precise measurement of the amount of adjustment needed, and the relationship of fixed asset investment to sales is seen as a gain in the utilization of plant capacity. Also, and perhaps for the first time, the management of operating debt is understood as the management of profit. Here, the increase in the turnover rate compared with plan indicates a substantial decrease in the level of current payables, indicating a possible prepayment of the acquisition of inventory, the price of which had included use of supplier credit for a longer period of time.

In terms of total capital employed, the Use of Capital report not only shows the excess amount used to produce the earnings, a factor which resulted in the net decrease in the rate of return, but also provides a measurement of *what the profit results would have been* if the planned turnover rate for the use of capital had been achieved:

Actual Sales	$11,500
Total Earnings	$ 700
Percent to Sales	6.1%
Budgeted Turnover Rate	2.0
Rate of Return on Capital	12.2%

From this calculation, it is but a short step to determine the profit impact of the excess capital employed, to determine how much of an increase would be required in the dollars of earnings to support the higher level of capital actually used and to yield the same potential rate of return. When used in this fashion, the gain or loss in profitability can then be measured directly from the Balance Sheet, a step which provides the final link needed in the measurement and management of profit, the focal point and end objective of business management itself.

Index